THE
GREEN GUIDE

Practical Steps To A Sustainable Lifestyle

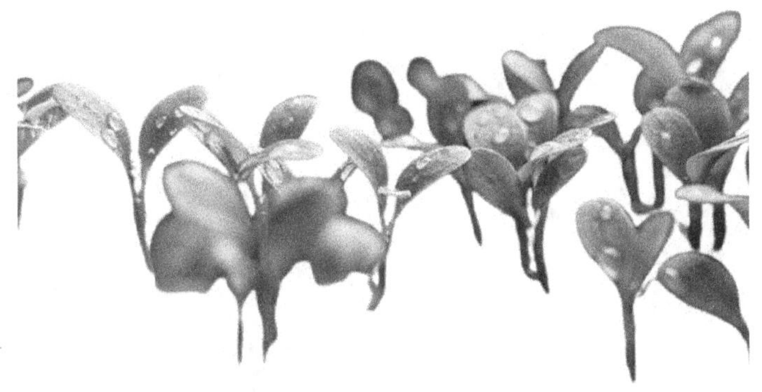

Susan Ribble

TABLE OF CONTENTS

INTRODUCTION

Welcome to a transformative journey towards a more sustainable and fulfilling lifestyle. In today's world, the impact of our choices on the environment has become increasingly clear. Every action we take, from the food we eat to the products we buy, has a ripple effect on our planet. This book, "The Green Guide: Practical Steps to a Sustainable Lifestyle," is here to help you navigate and embrace sustainable living, offering practical advice and actionable steps to make a positive difference.

Sustainability isn't just a buzzword—it's a crucial framework for ensuring that we can meet our current needs without compromising the ability of future generations to meet theirs. This approach balances environmental health, economic viability, and social well-being. By adopting sustainable practices, we contribute to preserving our planet's resources, improving our quality of life, and fostering a more equitable world for everyone.

"The Green Guide" is designed to be a comprehensive, user-friendly resource that you can refer to as you make your journey towards sustainability. This is the way you can capitalize on this book:

Start Where You Are: Whether you're a seasoned environmentalist or new to the concept of sustainability, this guide is for you. Begin with the sections that resonate most with your current lifestyle and interests.

Learn the Basics: Part 1: Understanding Sustainability provides essential background information. This foundation will help you grasp why sustainable living is important and how your actions can make a difference.

Implement Practical Steps: Each chapter offers practical advice and actionable steps. From greening your home and reducing waste to making eco-friendly purchases and travelling sustainably, you'll find a wealth of tips that you can start applying immediately.

Use Checklists and Tips: Throughout the book, you'll find checklists, tips, and real-life examples. These tools are designed to make your transition to a sustainable lifestyle straightforward and manageable.

Engage and Share: Sustainability thrives in community. Share your journey with friends, family, and neighbours.

Get involved in local environmental initiatives and inspire others to join you in making sustainable choices.

Reflect and Evolve: Sustainable living is an ongoing process. Regularly reflect on your habits, celebrate your successes, and stay open to learning and adapting. The more you integrate sustainable practices into your life, the more natural they will become.

By picking up this book, you're taking a significant step towards creating a healthier planet and a more sustainable future. Every small change you make adds up to a larger impact, contributing to a collective effort to protect our environment and improve our quality of life.

Thank you for setting out on this excursion with me. Let's work together to make sustainable living a reality, one step at a time.

CHAPTER ONE

What Is Sustainability?

Sustainability refers to the capacity to maintain or uphold conditions and practices that support the well-being of present and future generations. It encompasses the responsible use and management of natural resources, the preservation of ecological balance and biodiversity, the promotion of social equity and justice, and the fostering of economic prosperity—all while ensuring that these efforts do not compromise the ability of future generations to meet their own needs. In essence, sustainability operates on multiple levels, from individual actions to global policies and it involves finding a harmonious balance between environmental, social, and economic considerations to create a resilient and equitable society that can endure over the long term.

The Pillars Of Sustainability

Environmental Sustainability: At its core, environmental sustainability focuses on preserving and protecting natural ecosystems, resources, and biodiversity. It involves practices and policies aimed at conserving water, soil, air quality, forests, oceans, and other natural habitats. Key aspects include reducing pollution, minimizing waste, promoting renewable energy sources, and mitigating climate change impacts.

Social Sustainability: Social sustainability is concerned with promoting equity, justice, and well-being for all members of society. It emphasizes ensuring that basic human needs such as access to clean water, nutritious food, healthcare, education, and safe living conditions are met for everyone. Social sustainability also involves fostering inclusive communities, protecting human rights, supporting cultural diversity, and addressing issues of poverty, inequality, and social justice.

Economic Sustainability: Economic sustainability seeks to achieve prosperity and enhance living standards in a manner that is financially viable over the long term. It entails encouraging economic expansion that is fair, inclusive, and considerate of the environment. Economic sustainability requires efficient resource allocation, responsible consumption and production patterns, fair trade practices, and investments in sustainable infrastructure, innovation, and technology.

Overall, sustainability is about finding synergies and balance between environmental health, social equity, and economic prosperity. It requires integrating ecological, social, and economic considerations into decision-making processes at all levels, from individual lifestyle choices to corporate strategies and governmental policies. Embracing sustainability entails recognizing the interconnectedness of human and natural systems and working collaboratively to create a more resilient, equitable, and sustainable future for all.

The Current State of the Planet

The current state of the planet presents a complex and urgent set of challenges that require attention and action on multiple fronts.

Quite possibly of the most major problems confronting the planet today is climate change. Rising global temperatures, caused primarily by human activities such as burning fossil fuels and deforestation, are leading to more frequent and severe heat waves, storms, droughts, and other extreme weather events. Climate change threatens ecosystems, biodiversity, food security, water resources, and human health and well-being.

The planet is experiencing a rapid loss of biodiversity, with species extinction rates estimated to be tens to hundreds of times higher than the natural background rate. Habitat destruction, pollution, overexploitation of natural resources, invasive species, and climate change are among the main drivers of biodiversity loss. The decline in biodiversity has far-reaching consequences for ecosystem functioning, food security, and human livelihoods.

Pollution of air, water, and soil is a significant environmental challenge. Air pollution from vehicle emissions, industrial activities, and burning fossil fuels contributes to respiratory diseases and premature deaths. Water pollution from agricultural runoff, industrial discharge, and plastic waste threatens aquatic ecosystems and human health. Soil pollution affects agricultural productivity and food safety.

The unsustainable use of natural resources, including freshwater, forests, fisheries, and minerals, is depleting Earth's natural capital at an alarming rate. Overfishing, deforestation, soil degradation, and water scarcity are among the consequences of resource depletion. Unsustainable consumption and production patterns exacerbate these pressures on the planet's finite resources.

Environmental degradation, including deforestation, desertification, land degradation, and degradation of marine and coastal ecosystems, is widespread and accelerating in many parts of the world. These processes degrade habitats, reduce ecosystem services, and threaten the livelihoods of millions of people who depend on healthy ecosystems for food, water, and other resources.

Inequities in income, access to resources, and opportunities for education, healthcare, and employment contribute to social and economic disparities within and between countries. These inequities exacerbate vulnerability to environmental risks and climate change impacts, particularly for marginalized and disadvantaged communities.

Addressing these challenges requires concerted efforts at local, national, and global levels to promote sustainable development, conserve natural resources, mitigate climate change, protect biodiversity, and promote social equity and justice. It will require collaboration, innovation, and transformative change across all sectors of society to build a more resilient and sustainable future for people and the planet.

CHAPTER TWO

The Carbon Footprint Explained

The total amount of greenhouse gases, particularly carbon dioxide (CO2) and other carbon compounds, emitted by human activities, either directly or indirectly, is measured by the carbon footprint. It is expressed in terms of carbon dioxide equivalent (CO2e) and is typically measured in units of kilograms (kg) or metric tons (t) of CO2e per year.

Direct Emissions are emissions that occur directly from sources that are owned or controlled by an individual, organization, or entity. Examples include emissions from burning fossil fuels for heating, cooking, transportation (e.g., cars, trucks), and industrial processes. Direct emissions are relatively easy to measure and quantify.

Indirect Emissions (scope 2) are emissions associated with the generation of electricity, heat, or steam that is purchased or consumed by an individual or organization. They occur indirectly but are a consequence of the activities of the entity. Scope 2 emissions are typically measured based on the emissions intensity of the electricity or heat consumed.

Scope 3 are emissions that occur indirectly as a result of activities outside the direct control of an individual or organization but are associated with their activities across the entire supply chain. Scope 3 emissions can include emissions from purchased goods and services, business travel, employee commuting, waste disposal, and transportation of products.

To calculate the carbon footprint, one would typically:

Determine all sources of greenhouse gas emissions associated with the activities of interest, including direct emissions from fuel combustion and indirect emissions from purchased electricity, heat, and other goods and services.

Estimate the amount of greenhouse gases emitted from each source in terms of carbon dioxide equivalent (CO2e) using emission factors, conversion factors, or other relevant data.

Sum up the emissions from all sources to calculate the total carbon footprint. This may include emissions from Scope 1, Scope 2, and Scope 3 sources, depending on the scope of the analysis.

Report the carbon footprint in units of CO2e (e.g., kilograms or metric tons per year) and use it as a baseline to set reduction targets, track progress over time, and inform decision-making to mitigate climate change impacts.

Reducing carbon footprints typically involves implementing strategies to improve energy efficiency, switch to renewable energy sources, optimize transportation and logistics, reduce waste, and promote sustainable practices throughout the supply chain. By understanding and managing their carbon footprints, individuals, organizations, and governments can play a crucial role in mitigating climate change and transitioning to a low-carbon economy

How Everyday Actions Affect the Environment

Everyday actions, from the moment we wake up to the time we go to sleep, have profound and far-reaching effects on the environment. These actions collectively contribute to environmental degradation, climate change, and biodiversity loss.

Every time we turn on lights, use electronic devices, or heat our homes, we're tapping into energy sources that often come from fossil fuels. Burning coal, oil, and natural gas releases carbon dioxide (CO_2) and other greenhouse gases into the atmosphere, contributing to global warming and climate change. Energy production also requires the extraction of finite resources, such as coal mining or offshore drilling, which can have destructive impacts on ecosystems and wildlife habitats.

The water we use for drinking, bathing, washing clothes, and watering plants comes from freshwater sources like rivers, lakes, and aquifers. However, excessive water consumption, particularly in regions already facing water scarcity, can lead to depleted water supplies and ecosystem degradation. Moreover, pollution from agricultural runoff, industrial discharge, and untreated sewage can contaminate water bodies, making them unfit for human use and harming aquatic life.

Our consumption patterns contribute to the generation of vast amounts of waste, including packaging, plastics, electronics, and food scraps. Improper disposal of waste, such as littering or land filling, can pollute soil, water, and air. Plastics, in particular, pose a significant threat to marine life, as they can persist in the environment for hundreds of years, accumulating in oceans and harming marine ecosystems.

Whether we're commuting to work, driving to the grocery store, or flying for a vacation, transportation is a major source of greenhouse gas emissions and air pollution. Cars, trucks, airplanes, and ships burn fossil fuels, releasing pollutants such as carbon dioxide (CO2), nitrogen oxides (NOx), and particulate matter (PM) into the atmosphere. Urban sprawl and reliance on automobiles also contribute to habitat loss, biodiversity decline, and increased carbon emissions.

The food we eat has significant environmental implications, from the way it's produced to how it's transported and consumed. Agriculture, particularly livestock farming, is a major contributor to greenhouse gas emissions, deforestation, and water pollution. Additionally, food waste is a significant issue, as it not only squanders valuable resources like water and land but also generates methane emissions when it decomposes in landfills.

Our culture of consumerism drives demand for goods and products, leading to overconsumption of natural resources and production of excess waste. The extraction of raw materials, manufacturing processes, and transportation of goods all contribute to environmental degradation, including deforestation, habitat destruction, and pollution. Additionally, the disposal of products at the end of their lifecycle poses challenges for waste management and resource recovery.

Overall, the choices we make in our daily lives have profound implications for the health and sustainability of the planet. By adopting more sustainable practices, such as reducing energy consumption, conserving water, minimizing waste, using alternative transportation modes, making mindful food choices, and consuming less, We can work together to reduce our environmental impact and work toward a more sustainable future.

The Importance of Individual Action

Individual action is the cornerstone of meaningful change, serving as a catalyst for progress and a beacon of hope in a world facing daunting challenges.

Individual action empowers people to take control of their lives and surroundings. By making conscious choices in their daily lives, individuals demonstrate agency and initiative, showing that they have the power to effect change in their communities and beyond.

Collective action is built on the foundation of individual efforts. When individuals come together around a common cause, their collective impact can be transformative. A larger movement for positive change is made possible by every action, no matter how insignificant.

Individuals who take action inspire others to follow suit. By leading by example and demonstrating the benefits of sustainable living, activism, or philanthropy, individuals can motivate others to join in the effort to create a better world.

Individual actions influence policy decisions and cultural norms. Whether through advocacy, voting, or grassroots organizing, individuals have the power to shape public opinion and influence the direction of society.

Taking action aligns individuals with their values and sense of purpose, leading to personal fulfilment and a sense of accomplishment. Engaging in meaningful activities, whether it's volunteering, environmental stewardship, or social activism, can bring a profound sense of satisfaction and meaning to one's life.

Individual actions create a ripple effect that extends far beyond the immediate context. By sharing experiences, resources, and knowledge, individuals can amplify their impact and inspire change on a broader scale.

Individual actions contribute to building resilient communities and ecosystems. By adopting sustainable practices, preparing for emergencies, and fostering social connections, individuals can help communities adapt to challenges and thrive in the face of adversity.

Individuals who take action often drive innovation and creativity. Whether through entrepreneurial ventures, technological advancements, or artistic expression, individuals can inspire new ways of thinking and problem-solving that benefit society as a whole.

Individual actions leave a lasting legacy that extends beyond a single lifetime. By making a positive impact on the world, individuals can create a legacy of hope, compassion, and progress that inspires future generations to continue the work of building a better world.

In essence, individual action is the driving force behind positive change. By recognizing their power to make a difference and taking responsibility for their impact, individuals can help create a more just, sustainable, and equitable world for all.

CHAPTER THREE

Boosting Energy Efficiency in Your Home

Improving energy efficiency in your home is not only beneficial for reducing your carbon footprint and saving money on utility bills but also for enhancing comfort and indoor air quality. Here are some practical tips for boosting energy efficiency in your home:

- Install Energy Star-certified appliances in place of old, inefficient ones. Look for energy-efficient refrigerators, washing machines, dishwashers, and water heaters, which use significantly less energy than standard models.

- Programmable thermostats allow you to set heating and cooling schedules based on your daily routine. By automatically adjusting temperatures when you're away or asleep, you can reduce energy consumption and save on heating and cooling costs.

- Seal air leaks around doors, windows, and ducts to prevent drafts and heat loss. Adding insulation to attics, walls, and floors can further improve energy efficiency by minimizing heat transfer and maintaining comfortable indoor temperatures year-round.

- Switch to energy-efficient LED bulbs instead of CFLs and incandescent bulbs, which use less energy and last longer. LED lighting not only consumes less electricity but also produces less heat, keeping your home cooler during the summer.

- Plug electronics and appliances into smart power strips that automatically turn off power to devices when they're not in use. This prevents energy vampires from drawing standby power and helps reduce electricity waste.

- Make sure your heating, ventilation, and air conditioning (HVAC) systems get regular maintenance to make sure they work well. Regularly changing air filters, cleaning ducts, and tuning HVAC equipment will improve performance and extend its lifespan.

- Lower the temperature setting on your water heater to 120°F (49°C) to reduce energy consumption without sacrificing comfort. Insulate hot water pipes and consider installing a tank-less or heat pump water heater for greater energy efficiency.

- Consider installing solar panels on your roof to generate clean, renewable energy and offset electricity usage. Solar photovoltaic (PV) systems can significantly reduce or even eliminate your reliance on grid electricity, leading to long-term savings and environmental benefits.

- Adopt simple energy-saving habits such as turning off lights when not in use, unplugging electronics, using cold water for laundry, air-drying clothes, and limiting excessive heating and cooling. These little changes can amount to critical energy investment funds after some time.

By implementing these energy-efficient practices and upgrades in your home, you can lower your energy bills, reduce your environmental impact, and create a more comfortable and sustainable living space for you and your family.

Sustainable Heating and Cooling Solutions

In an era defined by environmental challenges and climate concerns, the quest for sustainable solutions has never been more urgent. One area ripe for transformation is heating and cooling systems in our homes and buildings. By harnessing the power of renewable energy, innovative technologies, and thoughtful design, sustainable heating and cooling offer a pathway to not only reduce our carbon footprint but also create healthier, more comfortable living spaces for all.

Sustainable heating and cooling systems leverage renewable energy sources such as solar, geothermal, and biomass to provide efficient and eco-friendly solutions. Solar thermal collectors harness the sun's energy to heat water or air for space heating and domestic hot water, offering a clean and abundant energy source. Geothermal heat pumps tap into the stable temperature of the earth to provide year-round heating and cooling, with minimal environmental impact.

Biomass heating systems utilize organic materials such as wood pellets or agricultural residues to generate heat, offering a renewable alternative to fossil fuels. By embracing these renewable energy sources, we can significantly reduce our reliance on finite resources and curb greenhouse gas emissions.

Innovative technologies play a key role in enhancing the efficiency and performance of sustainable heating and cooling systems. High-efficiency heat pumps, variable refrigerant flow systems, and radiant heating/cooling solutions optimize energy use and minimize waste. Smart thermostats and zoning controls allow for precise temperature management and customization, ensuring comfort while maximizing energy savings.

Energy recovery ventilation systems capture and transfer heat or coolness from exhaust air to incoming fresh air, improving indoor air quality and efficiency. These advancements in technology not only lower energy bills but also contribute to a healthier and more sustainable built environment.

Beyond technology, sustainable heating and cooling systems are rooted in thoughtful design principles that prioritize both comfort and sustainability. Passive design strategies such as proper insulation, passive solar heating, and natural ventilation optimize indoor comfort while reducing energy demand.

Energy-efficient building materials, high-performance windows, and airtight construction further enhance thermal performance and minimize heat loss. Integrating these design elements into new construction or renovations can transform buildings into energy-efficient, resilient, and sustainable spaces that benefit occupants and the planet alike.

As we confront the challenges of climate change and environmental degradation, the imperative to embrace sustainable heating and cooling solutions has never been clearer. By harnessing renewable energy, leveraging innovative technologies, and embracing thoughtful design, we can create homes and buildings that are not only comfortable and efficient but also environmentally responsible and resilient. Together, let us harness the power of nature's comfort to build a sustainable future for generations to come

Water Conservation Tips

Water, the elixir of life, sustains every living organism on our planet. Yet, as demand for this precious resource continues to rise and climate change exacerbates water scarcity, the need for water conservation has never been more urgent.

Before delving into conservation tips, it's crucial to understand our water footprint—the total volume of freshwater used to produce the goods and services we consume. By being mindful of our water footprint, we can make informed choices to reduce water consumption in our daily lives.

Addressing leaks and drips in our homes is a fundamental step in water conservation. A single leaking faucet can waste hundreds of gallons of water per year, so regularly check and repair leaks in faucets, toilets, and pipes to prevent water wastage.

Upgrading to water-efficient fixtures such as low-flow toilets, faucets, and showerheads can significantly reduce household water consumption without sacrificing comfort or functionality. These fixtures use less water per use while maintaining performance standards.

Adopt responsible watering practices in your garden or lawn by watering early in the morning or late in the evening to minimize evaporation. Utilize drip irrigation systems or soaker hoses to deliver water directly to plant roots and mulch garden beds to retain moisture.

Harness the power of nature by harvesting rainwater from your roof using rain barrels or cisterns. Collected rainwater can be used for outdoor irrigation, reducing the demand for potable water and conserving valuable resources.

Implement grey water recycling systems to reuse water from activities like laundry, dishwashing, or bathing for non-potable purposes such as toilet flushing or landscape irrigation. Grey water reuse reduces the strain on freshwater sources and promotes sustainability.

Adopt mindful consumption habits such as washing full loads of laundry and dishes, taking shorter showers, and turning off the tap while brushing teeth or shaving. Small changes in daily routines can add up to significant water savings over time.

Educate yourself and others about the importance of water conservation and advocate for sustainable water management practices in your community. Encourage the adoption of water-saving technologies and policies to protect and preserve our precious water resources for future generations.

In the face of mounting water challenges, every drop saved makes a difference.

CHAPTER FOUR

Non-Toxic Cleaning Solutions

In the pursuit of cleanliness and hygiene, the hidden dangers of conventional cleaning products are often overlooked. Laden with harsh chemicals and synthetic fragrances, these products pose significant risks to our health and the environment. Fortunately, non-toxic cleaning solutions offer a safer, effective, and eco-friendly alternative.

Conventional cleaning products often contain a mix of harsh chemicals, such as ammonia, chlorine bleach, phthalates, and volatile organic compounds (VOCs). These substances can cause a range of health issues, from respiratory problems and skin irritation to more severe conditions like endocrine disruption and carcinogenic effects. Additionally, the production and disposal of these chemicals contribute to environmental pollution, affecting water quality and marine life.

The Benefits of Non-Toxic Cleaning Solutions

Non-toxic cleaning solutions are made from natural ingredients that are safe for human health and the environment. Here are some key benefits:

- Healthier Indoor Air Quality: Non-toxic cleaners reduce indoor air pollution, decreasing the risk of respiratory issues and allergies.

- Safety for Vulnerable Populations: These products are safer for children, pets, and individuals with chemical sensitivities or chronic illnesses.

- Environmental Protection: Biodegradable and free from harmful chemicals, non-toxic cleaners minimize environmental impact, preserving water quality and wildlife.

- Cost-Effective: Many non-toxic cleaning solutions can be made from inexpensive household items, offering significant cost savings over commercial products.

Common Ingredients in Non-Toxic Cleaners

Understanding the ingredients used in non-toxic cleaning solutions is essential for creating effective and safe cleaners at home. Here are some common ingredients:

- Baking Soda: A natural abrasive and deodorizer, ideal for scrubbing surfaces and neutralizing odours.

- White Vinegar: An acid that effectively dissolves grease, mineral deposits, and grime. It also has antibacterial properties.

- Lemon Juice: A natural acid that cuts through grease and has antibacterial and antifungal properties.

- Castile Soap: A vegetable-based soap that is gentle yet effective at removing dirt and grime.

- Rejuvenating oils: Give regular aroma and have antimicrobial properties. Well known decisions incorporate tea tree oil, lavender oil, and eucalyptus oil.

- Hydrogen Peroxide: A mild disinfectant that can be used to sanitize surfaces and whiten laundry.

Tips for Transitioning to Non-Toxic Cleaning

Transitioning to non-toxic cleaning solutions can be straightforward with these tips:

- Start small by substituting non-toxic alternatives for one or two cleaning products, then work your way up.
- Read Labels: When purchasing commercial non-toxic cleaners, look for certifications such as USDA Organic, Green Seal, or EPA Safer Choice.
- Educate Household Members: Ensure everyone in your household understands the benefits of non-toxic cleaners and how to use them effectively.
- Stay Consistent: Make non-toxic cleaning a consistent practice by keeping DIY recipes and ingredients readily available.

Addressing Common Concerns and Misconceptions

Effectiveness: Non-toxic cleaning solutions are often perceived as less effective than their chemical-laden counterparts. However, when used correctly, natural ingredients like vinegar, baking soda, and essential oils can be just as effective at tackling dirt, grime, and bacteria.

Cost: While some non-toxic cleaning products may have a higher upfront cost, they often last longer and can be more economical in the long run. DIY solutions, in particular, are highly cost-effective.

Availability: With the growing demand for eco-friendly products, non-toxic cleaners are becoming increasingly available in stores and online. Additionally, many ingredients for DIY cleaners are common household items.

Embracing non-toxic cleaning solutions is a powerful way to protect your health, safeguard the environment, and create a safer home. By understanding the benefits, utilizing common natural ingredients, and incorporating simple DIY recipes, anyone can make the switch to greener cleaning practices.

As we move towards a more sustainable future, adopting non-toxic cleaning solutions is a small but significant step that contributes to the well-being of our planet and all its inhabitants. By making these changes, we can ensure that our homes are not only clean but also healthy and environmentally friendly.

Basic Recipes for a Greener Home

In an age where environmental consciousness is paramount, the products we use to clean our homes should reflect our commitment to sustainability. Numerous customary cleaning items contain hurtful synthetics that can adversely affect our wellbeing and the climate. Fortunately, Do-It-Yourself eco-accommodating cleaners offer a protected, compelling, and reasonable other option.

All-Purpose Cleaner

An all-purpose cleaner is a versatile solution that can be used on a variety of surfaces in your home, including countertops, appliances, and floors.

Ingredients:

- 1 cup white vinegar
- 1 cup water
- ten to fifteen drops of essential oil, such as lemon, tea tree, or lavender

Instructions:

- In a spray bottle, join the vinegar and water.
- Add the essential oil for fragrance and additional antibacterial properties.
- Shake well before each use.
- Use a cloth to clean surfaces after spraying it on them.

Glass and Mirror Cleaner

Keep your windows and mirrors sparkling clean without streaks using this simple and effective glass cleaner.

Ingredients:

- 1 cup water
- 1 cup white vinegar
- 1 tablespoon cornstarch

Instructions:

- Blend the water, vinegar, and cornstarch in a splash bottle.
- Give it a good shake to make sure the entire cornstarch is dissolved.

- Shower onto glass surfaces and wipe with microfiber fabric for a sans-streak sparkle.

Bathroom Scrub

This bathroom scrub is perfect for tackling soap scum, grime, and hard water stains in sinks, tubs, and tiles.

Ingredients:

- 1/2 cup baking soda
- 1/4 cup liquid Castile soap
- A few essential oil dabs (optional)

Instructions:

- Mix the baking soda and Castile soap in a bowl to form a thick paste.
- Add essential oil for fragrance whenever wanted.
- Apply the paste to surfaces using a sponge or brush.
- Scrub thoroughly and rinse with water.

Floor Cleaner

This floor cleaner is suitable for a variety of floor types, including tile, laminate, and hardwood.

Ingredients:

- 1/4 cup white vinegar

- 1 gallon hot water

- A few essential oil dabs(optional)

Instructions:

- Combine the vinegar and hot water in a bucket.

- Add medicinal ointment whenever wanted.

- Use a mop to clean the floors with the solution, wringing out excess liquid to avoid damaging wood floors.

Furniture Polish

Maintain the shine and health of your wooden furniture with this natural polish.

Ingredients:

- 1/4 cup olive oil

- 1/4 cup white vinegar

- 10 drops lemon essential oil

Instructions:

- Combine the olive oil and vinegar in a spray bottle.

- Add the lemon essential oil.

- Shake well before each use.

- Shower onto a delicate fabric and rub onto wooden surfaces in a round movement.

Laundry Detergent

This DIY laundry detergent is gentle on fabrics and effective at cleaning clothes without the use of harsh chemicals.

Ingredients:

- 1 bar of Castile soap, grated

- 1 cup washing soda

- 1 cup borax

Instructions:

- Grind the bar of Castile cleanser utilizing a cheddar grater.

- Mix the grated soap with washing soda and borax in a large bowl.

- Store the blend in a water/air proof compartment.

- Add one to two tablespoons to each heap of clothing.

Air Freshener

Freshen the air in your home with this natural and customizable air freshener.

Ingredients:

- 1 cup water
- 1 tablespoon baking soda
- 10-20 drops of medicinal oil (your decision)

Instructions:

- Dissolve the baking soda in water in a spray bottle.
- Add your preferred essential oil.
- Shake well before each use.
- Spray into the air as needed to eliminate odours.

Creating your own DIY eco-friendly cleaners is a simple yet powerful way to reduce your exposure to harmful chemicals, save money, and contribute to environmental sustainability. By using natural ingredients such as vinegar, baking soda, Castile soap, and essential oils, you can effectively clean your home while protecting your health and the planet. Embrace the green cleaning revolution and enjoy the benefits of a healthier, more eco-friendly living space.

Sustainable Household Goods

As awareness of environmental issues grows, more people are seeking ways to reduce their ecological footprint, starting with their homes. One effective approach is incorporating sustainable household goods. These products are designed to be eco-friendly, durable, and often ethically produced, contributing to a healthier planet and a more sustainable lifestyle.

Sustainable Kitchenware

The kitchen is a great place to start when transitioning to sustainable household goods. Many eco-friendly kitchen products are available that reduce waste and reliance on single-use items.

Reusable Food Storage:

Beeswax Wraps: These are a sustainable alternative to plastic wrap. Made from cotton infused with beeswax, they can be reused multiple times and are biodegradable.

Silicone Bags: Durable and versatile, silicone bags can be used for storing food, marinating, and even cooking. They replace single-use plastic bags and containers.

Eco-Friendly Cookware:

Cast Iron Pans: Long-lasting and highly durable, cast iron pans can last a lifetime with proper care, reducing the need for frequent replacements.

Bamboo Utensils: Bamboo is a fast-growing, renewable resource. Bamboo kitchen utensils are biodegradable and free from harmful chemicals found in some plastics.

Sustainable Cleaning Products

Switching to sustainable cleaning products can significantly reduce the number of harmful chemicals released into the environment and improve indoor air quality.

Non-Toxic Cleaners:

Eco-Friendly Brands: Look for cleaning products from brands that prioritize sustainability, such as Seventh Generation, E-cover, and Method. Natural ingredients and biodegradable make these products.

DIY Cleaners: Making your own cleaning solutions using ingredients like vinegar, baking soda, and essential oils is a cost-effective and eco-friendly alternative.

Reusable Cleaning Tools:

Microfiber Cloths: These cloths can be used multiple times and are effective at cleaning various surfaces without the need for chemical cleaners.

Wooden Scrub Brushes: Opt for brushes with natural bristles and wooden handles instead of plastic ones. They are biodegradable and often more durable.

Sustainable Personal Care Products

Plastic packaging is common for personal care products that contain harmful chemicals. Alternatives that are sustainable can have a positive impact on one's health and the environment.

Zero-Waste Personal Care:

Solid Shampoo Bars: These bars eliminate the need for plastic bottles and often contain natural, eco-friendly ingredients.

Reusable Cotton Rounds: Instead of single-use cotton pads, opt for reusable cotton rounds for applying toner or removing makeup. They can be used repeatedly after being cleaned.

Eco-Friendly Toiletries:

Bamboo Toothbrushes: Bamboo toothbrushes are biodegradable and a great alternative to plastic toothbrushes, which can take hundreds of years to decompose.

Natural Deodorants: Look for deodorants in recyclable packaging and made from natural ingredients to avoid harmful chemicals.

Sustainable Textiles

Textiles used in bedding, clothing, and home decor can have a significant environmental impact. Sustainable textiles offer a greener alternative.

Organic and Natural Fibres:

Organic Cotton: Grown without harmful pesticides and synthetic fertilizers, organic cotton is better for the environment and human health.

Linen: Made from the flax plant, linen is durable, biodegradable, and requires less water and pesticides to produce than cotton.

Recycled Materials:

Recycled Polyester: Items made from recycled polyester, such as blankets and clothing, help reduce waste and the demand for virgin materials.

Up-cycled Fabrics: Up-cycled textiles repurpose existing materials, reducing waste and the need for new resources.

Sustainable Home Furnishings

Furniture and home decor items can also be chosen with sustainability in mind to create an eco-friendly living space.

Eco-Friendly Furniture:

Second-Hand and Vintage: Buying second-hand or vintage furniture reduces waste and the demand for new materials.

Sustainable Wood: Using wood from sustainably managed forests helps protect ecosystems and reduces deforestation.

CHAPTER FIVE

A Comprehensive Guide to Reducing Waste

Effective recycling and composting offer tangible solutions to mitigate waste generation, conserve resources, and foster a greener future. This comprehensive guide delves into the principles, benefits, and practical steps of recycling and composting, empowering individuals to take meaningful action towards waste reduction and environmental stewardship.

Recycling is the process of converting used materials into new products, thereby reducing the need for virgin resources and minimizing environmental degradation. By separating recyclable items from general waste and facilitating their reprocessing, recycling conserves energy, reduces greenhouse gas emissions, and lessens the burden on landfills.

Key recyclable materials include paper, plastics, glass, metals, and electronics, each requiring specific handling to maximize recovery and reuse.

Understanding the different types of recyclables and their collection methods is essential. From paper and plastics to metals and electronics, each material has its unique recycling process and requirements. Proper recycling practices ensure the efficiency and effectiveness of the recycling process. This includes cleaning and sorting recyclables, avoiding contamination, and following local recycling guidelines.

Effective Composting

The natural process of composting turns organic waste into compost, which adds nutrients to the soil. It involves the breakdown of organic matter by microorganisms under controlled conditions. Composting not only reduces landfill waste but also improves soil health, increases fertility, and sequesters carbon dioxide from the atmosphere.

Composting offers numerous benefits, including the reduction of methane emissions from landfills, the enrichment of soil with organic nutrients, and the diversion of organic waste from disposal sites. Identifying what can and cannot be composted is crucial for successful composting. Organic materials such as fruit and vegetable scraps, coffee grounds, and yard waste are suitable for composting, while items like meat, dairy, and synthetic materials should be avoided.

Various composting methods, including backyard composting, vermin-composting (using worms), and bokashi composting (using fermented bran), offer flexibility and versatility to suit different lifestyles and living situations.

Despite the benefits of recycling and composting, several challenges may hinder their effectiveness. Common challenges include recycling contamination, composting odours and pests, and lack of awareness or infrastructure. By addressing these challenges through education, community involvement, and proactive solutions, individuals can enhance the success of their recycling and composting efforts.

Effective recycling and composting are essential practices for reducing waste, conserving resources, and mitigating environmental impact. By embracing these practices in their daily lives, individuals can make a meaningful contribution to a more sustainable future. This comprehensive guide serves as a roadmap for individuals seeking to reduce waste through recycling and composting, empowering them to take action and become stewards of the environment. For future generations, we can create a world that is cleaner, greener, and more sustainable together.

Reducing Single-Use Plastics: A Pathway to a Cleaner Future

In this day and age, the omnipresent presence of single-use plastics has turned into a squeezing natural concern. From shopping bags to water bottles, these disposable items have permeated every aspect of our daily lives, leading to staggering amounts of plastic waste polluting our oceans, harming wildlife, and endangering ecosystems. However, by adopting simple yet impactful strategies, we can work towards breaking free from the cycle of single-use plastics, paving the way for a more sustainable future.

Before we can effectively tackle the issue of single-use plastics, it's crucial to comprehend the scope of the problem. Each year, millions of tons of single-use plastics are produced worldwide, with only a fraction being recycled. The rest end up in landfills, incinerators, or as litter in our environment, where they can take hundreds of years to decompose, releasing harmful chemicals in the process. This cycle of consumption and disposal is not only unsustainable but also poses significant risks to human health and the planet.

The first step towards reducing single-use plastics is to rethink our consumption habits. This involves being mindful of the products we buy and opting for alternatives that are more sustainable and eco-friendly. For instance, instead of using plastic bags at the grocery store, bring reusable cloth bags or tote bags. Similarly, invest in a durable, refillable water bottle rather than buying bottled water. By making conscious choices and reducing our reliance on single-use plastics, we can significantly decrease our environmental footprint.

In addition to reducing consumption, embracing reusable alternatives is key to minimizing single-use plastics in our daily lives. Switching to reusable items such as stainless steel straws, glass containers, and bamboo utensils can help eliminate the need for disposable plastics. Not only are these eco-friendly alternatives better for the environment, but they are also frequently longer-lasting and less expensive over time. By making small changes in our habits and embracing reusable solutions, we can make a big difference in reducing plastic waste.

Another effective way to reduce single-use plastics is to support plastic-free initiatives and advocate for policy changes at the local, national, and global levels. This can include supporting legislation that bans or regulates the production and distribution of single-use plastics, as well as encouraging businesses to adopt more sustainable practices. Additionally, participating in community clean-up efforts and spreading awareness about the importance of reducing plastic waste can help mobilize collective action and drive positive change.

Lastly, education plays a crucial role in addressing the issue of single-use plastics. By raising awareness about the environmental impacts of plastic pollution and providing practical tips for reducing plastic waste, we can empower individuals and communities to take action. Whether through educational campaigns, workshops, or social media outreach, sharing information and resources can inspire others to join the movement towards a plastic-free future.

Reducing single-use plastics is not just a personal choice but a collective responsibility that requires concerted efforts from individuals, businesses, and governments alike. By rethinking our consumption habits, embracing reusable alternatives, supporting plastic-free initiatives, and educating others, we can work towards breaking free from the grip of single-use plastics and creating a more sustainable and resilient planet for future generations. Together, let's make the switch from disposable to durable and pave the way for a cleaner, greener future.

CHAPTER SIX

The Benefits of a Plant-Based Diet

In recent years, the popularity of plant-based diets has surged as more people recognize the numerous health benefits and environmental advantages they offer. Unlike traditional diets centred around animal products, plant-based diets focus on whole, minimally processed foods derived from plants, such as fruits, vegetables, grains, legumes, nuts, and seeds. By embracing this dietary approach, individuals can not only improve their own well-being but also contribute to a more sustainable and compassionate food system.

Promotes Heart Health:

One of the essential advantages of a plant-based diet is its positive effect on heart wellbeing. Plant-based foods are naturally low in saturated fat and cholesterol, making them ideal for reducing the risk of cardiovascular diseases such as heart attacks, strokes, and hypertension. Additionally, the high fibre content found in fruits, vegetables, and whole grains helps to lower cholesterol levels, stabilize blood sugar, and improve overall heart function, leading to a healthier cardiovascular system.

Supports Weight Management:

Another advantage of a plant-based diet is its effectiveness in supporting weight management and promoting healthy weight loss. Plant-based foods are typically lower in calories and higher in fibre compared to animal products, which can help individuals feel fuller for longer and reduce overeating. By focusing on nutrient-dense plant foods and minimizing processed foods and added sugars, individuals can achieve and maintain a healthy weight more easily, leading to improved overall well-being and reduced risk of obesity-related conditions.

Enhances Digestive Health:

Plant-based diets are rich in fibre, vitamins, minerals, and antioxidants, all of which contribute to better digestive health. Fibre, in particular, plays a crucial role in promoting regular bowel movements, preventing constipation, and maintaining a healthy gut micro-biome. Diverticulitis, inflammatory bowel disease and colorectal cancer are just a few of the digestive conditions that can be lessened by consuming a variety of plant-based foods, which can support the growth of beneficial gut bacteria.

Reduces Risk of Chronic Diseases:

Numerous studies have shown that plant-based diets are associated with a lower risk of chronic diseases, including type 2 diabetes, certain types of cancer, and neurodegenerative conditions. The abundance of vitamins, minerals, antioxidants, and phyto-nutrients found in plant foods helps to reduce inflammation, neutralize free radicals, and support immune function, thereby reducing the risk of developing these diseases. By prioritizing plant-based foods in their diet, individuals can improve their long-term health outcomes and increase their longevity.

Benefits the Environment:

In addition to the health benefits, adopting a plant-based diet also has significant environmental advantages. Deforestation, water pollution, habitat destruction, and emissions of greenhouse gases are all primarily caused by animal agriculture. By choosing plant-based foods over animal products, individuals can reduce their carbon footprint, conserve natural resources, and mitigate the environmental impact of food production. Transitioning to a plant-based diet is one of the most effective ways for individuals to contribute to global sustainability efforts and combat climate change.

The benefits of a plant-based diet are vast and far-reaching, encompassing improvements in personal health, environmental sustainability, and animal welfare. By embracing a diet rich in fruits, vegetables, grains, legumes, nuts, and seeds, individuals can enjoy a myriad of health benefits, including better heart health, weight management, digestive function, and reduced risk of chronic diseases. Furthermore, by reducing reliance on animal products, individuals can play a significant role in protecting the planet and creating a more sustainable food system for future generations. Ultimately, adopting a plant-based diet is not just a dietary choice but a lifestyle change that can lead to a healthier, happier living.

Sustainable Food Choices: Nourishing Our Bodies, Protecting Our Planet

In an era marked by environmental challenges and growing concerns about food security, the importance of sustainable food choices cannot be overstated. The way we produce, distribute, and consume food has profound implications for both our health and the health of the planet. By making informed decisions about what we eat, we have the power to promote sustainability, support local economies, and mitigate the impacts of climate change.

At its core, sustainable food choices are about fostering food systems that are environmentally responsible, socially just, and economically viable. This means considering the entire lifecycle of food production, from farm to fork, and minimizing its ecological footprint. Sustainable food systems prioritize practices such as organic farming, water conservation, biodiversity preservation, and fair labour practices, all of which contribute to long-term environmental and social sustainability.

One of the most impactful ways to promote sustainability in our food choices is by embracing plant-based diets. Plant-based diets centre around whole, minimally processed foods derived from plants, such as fruits, vegetables, grains, legumes, nuts, and seeds. By reducing our consumption of animal products and incorporating more plant-based foods into our diets, we can significantly reduce greenhouse gas emissions, conserve water and land resources, and mitigate deforestation associated with livestock farming.

Another key aspect of sustainable food choices is supporting local and seasonal foods. By purchasing food from local farmers and producers, we can reduce the carbon footprint associated with transportation and support the local economy. Additionally, choosing seasonal foods helps to minimize the energy and resources required for production and storage, as well as promotes biodiversity and culinary diversity.

Addressing food waste is essential for promoting sustainability in our food systems. Globally, one-third of all food produced for human consumption is wasted each year, contributing to greenhouse gas emissions and resource depletion. By practicing mindful shopping, meal planning, proper storage, and creative cooking techniques, we can minimize food waste at home and support efforts to achieve a more efficient and equitable food system.

In addition to individual actions, advocating for policy change is critical for advancing sustainable food systems on a larger scale. This can include supporting initiatives that promote sustainable agriculture, improve food access and affordability, regulate food labelling and marketing, and incentivize environmentally friendly practices. By engaging with policymakers and participating in advocacy efforts, we can help shape policies that prioritize sustainability, equity, and resilience in our food systems.

Strategies for Reducing Food Waste and Building Sustainable Communities"

In a world where millions suffer from hunger and environmental degradation threatens our planet, the issue of food waste demands urgent attention. Each year, billions of tons of food are wasted globally, exacerbating hunger, squandering valuable resources, and contributing to greenhouse gas emissions. However, by adopting innovative solutions and changing our behaviours, we can significantly reduce food waste and build more sustainable communities.

The first step in addressing food waste is raising awareness about its prevalence and impacts. Many people are unaware of the staggering amount of food wasted each day and the environmental, social, and economic consequences it entails. By educating individuals, businesses, and communities about the importance of reducing food waste, we can foster a culture of mindfulness and responsibility towards our food resources.

Effective meal planning and preparation are key strategies for minimizing food waste at home. By creating shopping lists, cooking in batch, and storing leftovers properly, we can ensure that food is used efficiently and not left to spoil. Additionally, learning to repurpose ingredients and use kitchen scraps creatively can help maximize the use of food resources and minimize waste.

Food recovery initiatives play a vital role in diverting surplus food from landfills and redistributing it to those in need. Organizations such as food banks, shelters, and community kitchens work tirelessly to rescue edible food that would otherwise go to waste and provide it to individuals and families facing food insecurity. By supporting and volunteering with food recovery organizations, we can help bridge the gap between surplus food and hunger while reducing waste.

Policy interventions are crucial for addressing food waste at a systemic level. Governments and policymakers can enact regulations and incentives to encourage food waste reduction throughout the supply chain, from production and distribution to retail and consumption. This can include measures such as standardized date labelling, tax incentives for food donation, and mandatory composting programs. By advocating for policy changes and holding stakeholders accountable, we can create an enabling environment for reducing food waste.

Addressing food waste requires collaboration and innovation across sectors and stakeholders. Businesses, governments, nonprofits, and individuals must work together to develop and implement scalable solutions that tackle food waste holistically. This can involve investing in infrastructure for food recovery and composting, adopting technologies for tracking and optimizing food supply chains, and supporting research and development of sustainable packaging and preservation methods. By fostering a culture of collaboration and innovation, we can unlock new opportunities for reducing food waste and building more resilient food systems.

Reducing food waste is not just a moral imperative but also a strategic imperative for building sustainable communities and addressing global challenges such as hunger and climate change. By raising awareness, planning and preparing meals mindfully, supporting food recovery initiatives, advocating for policy changes, and fostering collaboration and innovation, we can make significant progress towards a future where waste is minimized, resources are optimized, and everyone has access to nutritious food. Together, let's waste not, want not, and create a more equitable and sustainable world for all.

CHAPTER SEVEN

Making Sustainable Style Choices for a Greener Future

As the fashion industry continues to evolve, so too does our understanding of its environmental and social impacts. From resource depletion and pollution to labour exploitation and waste generation, the conventional fashion system poses significant challenges to sustainability. However, by making informed choices and embracing sustainable fashion practices, we can transform the way we dress and contribute to a more ethical and environmentally conscious industry.

The fashion industry is one of the largest and most polluting industries in the world, with a complex supply chain that spans production, distribution, and consumption. From the cultivation of raw materials to the manufacturing of garments and their eventual disposal, each stage of the fashion lifecycle carries environmental and social implications. By understanding the environmental and social impacts of fashion, we can make more conscious choices about the clothes we buy and wear.

One of the most impactful ways to support sustainability in fashion is by choosing brands that prioritize ethical and transparent practices. Look for brands that prioritize fair labour conditions, pay living wages to workers, and prioritize sustainable materials and production methods. Many brands now provide transparency reports detailing their environmental and social performance, allowing consumers to make more informed decisions about where they shop.

Another key aspect of sustainable fashion is investing in quality, timeless pieces that are designed to last. Instead of chasing fleeting trends and disposable fashion, opt for well-made garments that are durable, versatile, and timeless in style. By choosing quality over quantity, we can reduce our consumption and minimize the environmental impact of our wardrobes.

Circular fashion initiatives are revolutionizing the way we produce, consume, and dispose of clothing. By promoting practices such as clothing rental, resale, and repair, circular fashion aims to extend the lifecycle of garments and minimize waste. Support initiatives that encourage circularity in fashion, such as clothing rental platforms, resale marketplaces, and repair cafes. By embracing circular fashion, we can reduce our environmental footprint and contribute to a more sustainable fashion industry.

At its core, sustainable fashion is about consuming less and making more conscious choices about what we buy and wear. Embrace minimalism by curating a wardrobe of essential pieces that bring joy and serve multiple purposes. Consider the item's impact on the environment and society before making a purchase. Ask yourself if you really need it. By practicing conscious consumption, we can reduce our reliance on fast fashion and promote a more sustainable fashion culture.

Sustainable fashion is not just a trend but a movement towards a more ethical, equitable, and environmentally conscious industry. By understanding the impact of fashion, embracing ethical and transparent brands, investing in quality and timeless pieces, supporting circular fashion initiatives, and practicing minimalism and conscious consumption, The fashion industry can benefit from our efforts. Together, let's redefine fashion as a force for good and pave the way for a greener, fairer future.

Ethical and Eco-Friendly Beauty Products

In the pursuit of beauty, it's essential to consider not only the effectiveness of the products we use but also their ethical and environmental impact. The beauty industry, like many others, has historically been associated with practices that harm the planet and exploit workers. However, a growing movement towards ethical and eco-friendly beauty products is reshaping the industry, offering consumers options that prioritize sustainability, transparency, and social responsibility.

The beauty industry has a significant environmental footprint, from the extraction of raw materials to the manufacturing of products and their eventual disposal. Many beauty products contain harmful chemicals that can pollute waterways and harm ecosystems, while packaging waste contributes to landfill accumulation. Additionally, unethical labour practices, such as forced labour and child labour, are prevalent in the beauty supply chain. By understanding the industry's impact, we can make more informed choices about the products we use.

One way to support ethical and eco-friendly beauty is by choosing products made with clean and natural ingredients. Look for products that are free from harmful chemicals such as parabens, phthalates, and sulfates, and instead contain plant-based, organic, or sustainably sourced ingredients. Many brands now offer transparency about their ingredient sourcing and production processes, allowing consumers to make more informed choices about the products they purchase.

Animal testing is a widespread practice in the beauty industry, but it's also one that's increasingly being challenged by consumers who demand cruelty-free alternatives. Look for beauty brands that are certified cruelty-free by organizations such as Leaping Bunny or PETA, meaning they do not test their products or ingredients on animals. Additionally, consider supporting vegan beauty brands that do not use animal-derived ingredients in their products, further reducing harm to animals and the environment.

Packaging waste is a significant issue in the beauty industry, with billions of plastic containers ending up in landfills each year. Look for brands that prioritize sustainable packaging alternatives, such as recyclable, biodegradable, or refillable containers. Some brands even offer innovative packaging solutions, such as compostable materials or packaging-free products. By choosing products with minimal packaging or packaging that can be recycled or repurposed, we can reduce our environmental impact and support a circular economy.

In addition to ingredient sourcing and packaging, it's essential to consider the broader ethical and social practices of beauty brands. Look for brands that prioritize fair labour practices, pay living wages to workers, and support communities where ingredients are sourced. Many brands now provide transparency reports detailing their environmental and social performance, allowing consumers to make more informed choices about where they spend their money.

Ethical and eco-friendly beauty products offer a way to indulge in self-care while also supporting values of sustainability, transparency, and social responsibility. By choosing products made with clean and natural ingredients, supporting cruelty-free and vegan brands, prioritizing sustainable packaging, and supporting ethical and transparent brands, we can make a positive impact on the beauty industry and the planet. Together, let's embrace beauty that radiates from the inside out – one that nourishes not only our skin but also our conscience and the world around us.

The Impact of Fast Fashion

In today's consumer culture, fast fashion has become synonymous with affordability, accessibility, and trendiness. However, behind the glossy facade lies a dark reality of environmental degradation, exploitation of labour, and social inequality. The exponential growth of fast fashion brands has led to a throwaway culture that prioritizes profit over people and planet, perpetuating a cycle of overconsumption and waste with far-reaching consequences.

Environmental Degradation:

Fast fashion's reliance on cheap, disposable garments comes at a staggering environmental cost. From the intensive cultivation of cotton and other raw materials to the toxic chemicals used in dyeing and finishing processes, fast fashion production wreaks havoc on ecosystems and contributes to air and water pollution. Additionally, the vast quantities of clothing produced and discarded each year contribute to landfill overflow and greenhouse gas emissions, exacerbating climate change and environmental degradation.

Exploitation of Labour:

Behind every cheap garment is a hidden human cost. The fast fashion industry relies heavily on low-wage labour in developing countries, where workers, predominantly women, toil in unsafe conditions and for meagre wages. Sweatshops and garment factories often violate basic labour rights, subjecting workers to long hours, unsafe working conditions, and minimal pay. Furthermore, the pressure to meet fast fashion's relentless demand for quick turnaround times often leads to exploitative labour practices and worker abuses.

Social Inequality:

Fast fashion perpetuates social inequality both globally and locally. In developing countries, the exploitation of cheap labour perpetuates cycles of poverty and economic dependency, trapping workers in a cycle of exploitation with few opportunities for upward mobility. Moreover, fast fashion's emphasis on cheap, disposable clothing undermines traditional textile industries in developing countries, further exacerbating economic disparities. Locally, the rise of fast fashion has led to the decline of local garment industries and the loss of skilled labour jobs in many communities.

Disposable Culture:

At the heart of fast fashion lies a culture of disposability, where clothing is treated as a fleeting trend rather than a long-term investment. The rapid turnover of styles and the pressure to constantly update one's wardrobe contribute to a cycle of overconsumption and waste. Many garments are worn only a few times before being discarded, leading to a mountain of textile waste that overwhelms landfills and incinerators. This disposable culture not only wastes valuable resources but also perpetuates unsustainable consumption patterns and a disconnect from the true value of clothing.

As awareness of the dark side of fast fashion grows, so too does the call for change. Consumers are increasingly demanding transparency, accountability, and ethical practices from fashion brands. A growing number of ethical and sustainable fashion brands are emerging, offering alternatives to the fast fashion model. Additionally, initiatives promoting clothing rental, second-hand shopping, and up-cycling are gaining traction, encouraging consumers to rethink their relationship with fashion and embrace more conscious consumption habits.

The impact of fast fashion extends far beyond the clothing racks, affecting ecosystems, communities, and individuals around the world. As consumers, we have the power to demand change and reshape the fashion industry into one that values people and planet over profit. By supporting ethical and sustainable fashion brands, embracing conscious consumption habits, and advocating for systemic change, we can build a fashion industry that is fair, transparent, and environmentally responsible. Together, let's redefine fashion as a force for good and pave the way for a more sustainable and equitable future.

CHAPTER EIGHT

Responsible Shopping and Consumerism

In a world where consumerism reigns supreme, the act of shopping has profound implications for both individuals and the planet. From the products we buy to the companies we support, every purchase we make shapes the world around us. By adopting a mindset of responsible shopping and consumerism, we can harness our purchasing power to create positive change, promote sustainability, and support ethical practices.

Conscious Consumption:

At the heart of responsible shopping is conscious consumption – the practice of making deliberate and informed choices about what we buy and why. Instead of mindlessly succumbing to the lure of consumer culture, take the time to consider the environmental, social, and ethical implications of each purchase. Ask yourself if you truly need the item, if it aligns with your values, and if there are more sustainable alternatives available. By adopting a mindset of conscious consumption, we can reduce our environmental footprint and minimize the negative impact of our purchasing decisions.

Prioritizing Quality Over Quantity:

In a world of fast fashion and disposable goods, prioritizing quality over quantity is key to responsible shopping. Instead of chasing the latest trends and accumulating possessions, invest in well-made, durable products that are built to last. While high-quality items may come with a higher price tag upfront, they often save money in the long run by lasting longer and requiring fewer replacements. Additionally, choosing quality over quantity helps reduce waste and minimize the environmental impact of our consumption.

Supporting Ethical and Sustainable Brands:

Where we choose to spend our money matters. Support brands and companies that prioritize ethical and sustainable practices, such as fair labour conditions, environmentally friendly production methods, and transparent supply chains. Look for certifications and labels that indicate a commitment to sustainability, such as Fair Trade, Organic, or B Corp certification. By supporting ethical and sustainable brands, we can drive demand for responsible products and encourage positive change within the industry.

Embracing Second-Hand and Circular Shopping:

One of the most effective ways to reduce our environmental impact is by embracing second-hand and circular shopping. Instead of always buying new, consider purchasing pre-owned or vintage items from thrift stores, consignment shops, or online marketplaces. Not only does buying second-hand extend the lifecycle of products and reduce waste, but it also often offers unique and affordable finds. Additionally, participate in clothing swaps, rental programs, and repair initiatives to further promote a circular economy and minimize resource consumption.

Practicing Gratitude and Minimalism:

Consumerism thrives on the idea of more, more, more – but true fulfilment often comes from less. Embrace minimalism by de-cluttering your life and letting go of excess possessions that no longer serve you. Practice gratitude for what you have and cultivate a mindset of contentment and appreciation for the things that truly matter. By focusing on experiences, relationships, and personal growth rather than material possessions, we can break free from the cycle of consumerism and find greater fulfilment in life.

Responsible shopping and consumerism are about more than just what we buy – they're about the values we uphold and the world we want to create. By adopting a mindset of conscious consumption, prioritizing quality over quantity, supporting ethical and sustainable brands, embracing second-hand and circular shopping, and practicing gratitude and minimalism, we can make a meaningful impact on the planet and promote a more sustainable and equitable future. Together, let's use our purchasing power for good and create a world where every shopping choice counts.

CHAPTER NINE

Green Travel and Transportation

Travel broadens our horizons, but traditional modes of transportation can have a significant environmental impact. Fortunately, a growing movement towards green travel and transportation offers alternatives that prioritize sustainability, reduce carbon emissions, and minimize ecological footprint. By embracing sustainable practices and innovations, we can explore the world responsibly while preserving it for future generations.

One of the most effective ways to reduce our carbon footprint while travelling is to choose sustainable transportation options. Instead of relying on fossil fuel-powered vehicles, consider alternatives such as public transit, walking, cycling, or electric vehicles. Public transportation networks are increasingly available in many destinations, offering convenient and eco-friendly ways to get around. Additionally, walking and cycling not only reduce emissions but also allow travellers to immerse themselves in local culture and scenery.

Where we choose to stay can also have a significant impact on our environmental footprint. Look for eco-friendly accommodations that prioritize sustainability in their operations, such as energy and water conservation, waste reduction, and use of renewable resources.

Many hotels and resorts now offer green certifications or eco-labels to help travellers identify environmentally responsible options. Additionally, consider alternative lodging options such as eco-lodges, hostels, or home stays, which often have lower environmental impact and provide unique cultural experiences.

While travelling, it's important to be mindful of our consumption habits and minimize waste. Bring reusable water bottles, shopping bags, and utensils to reduce reliance on single-use plastics. Opt for local, seasonal, and sustainably sourced food options to support the local economy and reduce food miles. Choose experiences that prioritize cultural and environmental conservation, such as wildlife watching, nature hikes, and cultural tours. By minimizing waste and consumption, we can reduce our environmental impact and leave destinations as pristine as we found them.

Despite our best efforts to minimize emissions, travel often involves unavoidable carbon emissions. To mitigate the environmental impact of our journeys, consider offsetting carbon emissions through reputable carbon offset programs. These programs invest in projects that reduce or capture greenhouse gas emissions, such as reforestation, renewable energy, and energy efficiency initiatives. By investing in carbon offsets, travellers can balance out the emissions associated with their travel and contribute to global efforts to combat climate change.

Beyond individual actions, supporting sustainable tourism practices is essential for promoting responsible travel on a broader scale. Choose tour operators, travel agencies, and destinations that prioritize sustainability, community engagement, and cultural preservation. Look for certifications and memberships, such as Ecotourism certifications or memberships in sustainable tourism organizations, which indicate a commitment to responsible tourism practices. Additionally, advocate for policies and regulations that promote sustainable tourism development and protect natural and cultural heritage sites for future generations to enjoy.

Green travel and transportation offer opportunities to explore the world responsibly while minimizing our environmental impact. By embracing sustainable transportation options, choosing eco-friendly accommodations, minimizing waste and consumption, offsetting carbon emissions, and supporting sustainable tourism practices, we can make a positive difference in the places we visit and the planet as a whole. Together, let's embark on journeys that not only enrich our lives but also preserve the beauty and diversity of our world for generations to come.

The Effects of Different Transportation Options on the Environment

Transportation assumes a significant part in current culture, associating individuals, products, and thoughts across huge distances. However, the environmental impact of transportation can vary significantly depending on the mode of transport used. By understanding the environmental implications of different transportation options, we can make informed choices that prioritize sustainability and minimize harm to the planet.

Automobiles:

Cars are one of the most common modes of transportation worldwide, but they also have a significant environmental footprint. Internal combustion engines powered by fossil fuels emit greenhouse gases such as carbon dioxide (CO_2), contributing to climate change and air pollution. Additionally, cars require vast amounts of land for roads and parking, leading to habitat destruction and urban sprawl. While advancements in fuel efficiency and electric vehicles offer some promise, widespread adoption of sustainable transportation alternatives is essential to reduce the environmental impact of automobile travel.

Public Transit:

Public transit systems, including buses, trains, and subways, offer a more sustainable alternative to individual car travel. By consolidating passengers into shared vehicles, public transit reduces the number of vehicles on the road and decreases greenhouse gas emissions per capita. Additionally, many public transit systems are electrifying their fleets or transitioning to renewable energy sources, further reducing environmental impact. Investing in robust public transit infrastructure and promoting its use can help alleviate congestion, reduce emissions, and enhance urban liveability.

Cycling and Walking:

Cycling and walking are among the most environmentally friendly modes of transportation available. They produce zero emissions, require minimal infrastructure, and promote physical activity and community engagement. However, the feasibility of cycling and walking as primary modes of transport depends on factors such as urban design, safety infrastructure, and accessibility. Investing in bike lanes, pedestrian-friendly streets, and mixed-use development can encourage active transportation and create more sustainable, liveable cities.

Air Travel:

Air travel is a convenient but highly carbon-intensive mode of transportation, particularly for long-distance travel. Commercial airplanes emit large quantities of greenhouse gases, including CO_2 and nitrogen oxides (NOx), which contribute to climate change and air pollution. Additionally, the growth of air travel has led to concerns about noise pollution, habitat disruption, and biodiversity loss around airports. While technological advancements such as more fuel-efficient aircraft and sustainable aviation fuels show promise, reducing the environmental impact of air travel will require a combination of technological innovation, policy intervention, and behavioural change.

Shipping and Freight:

Maritime shipping and freight transport play a vital role in global trade and commerce, but they also have significant environmental impacts. Cargo ships and freight trucks emit greenhouse gases, air pollutants, and marine debris, contributing to climate change, air pollution, and ocean pollution. Additionally, the expansion of ports and shipping lanes can lead to habitat destruction, coastal erosion, and disruption of marine ecosystems. Implementing measures such as slow steaming, fuel efficiency standards, and emission control technologies can help mitigate the environmental impact of shipping and freight transport.

The environmental impact of transportation varies widely depending on the mode of transport used. While some modes, such as cars and airplanes, are highly carbon-intensive and resource-intensive, others, such as public transit, cycling, and walking, offer more sustainable alternatives. By promoting sustainable transportation options, investing in infrastructure and technology, and encouraging behavioural change, we can create a transportation system that is both efficient and environmentally responsible. Together, let's navigate the road to sustainability and build a greener, more sustainable future for all.

Tips for Sustainable Travel

Travelling offers the opportunity to explore new cultures, landscapes, and experiences, but it's essential to do so in a way that minimizes our environmental impact and supports local communities. By adopting sustainable travel practices, we can enjoy unforgettable adventures while preserving the planet for future generations. Here are some tips for eco-conscious travellers looking to explore the world responsibly.

Choose Sustainable Accommodations:

Opt for eco-friendly accommodations that prioritize sustainability in their operations. Look for hotels, resorts, and lodges that have implemented energy-saving measures, such as solar panels, LED lighting, and water-saving fixtures. Additionally, consider staying at eco-lodges, home stays, or sustainable tourism initiatives that support local communities and minimize environmental impact.

Pack Light and Smart:

Pack light to reduce fuel consumption and carbon emissions associated with transportation. Choose versatile, multi-purpose clothing and pack reusable items such as water bottles, shopping bags, and utensils to minimize waste. Additionally, consider eco-friendly toiletries and personal care products, such as biodegradable soaps and shampoos, to reduce the environmental impact of your travels.

Minimize Carbon Emissions:

Opt for low-carbon transportation options whenever possible. Choose trains, buses, or shared transportation over individual car rentals or flights for shorter distances. When flying is necessary, consider non-stop flights and carbon offset programs to mitigate the environmental impact of air travel. Additionally, explore alternative modes of transportation such as cycling, walking, or electric scooters for exploring local destinations.

Support Local Communities:

Support local economies and communities by patronizing locally-owned businesses, restaurants, and artisans. Choose experiences that provide authentic cultural immersion and support traditional crafts and practices. Engage with local guides and tour operators who are knowledgeable about the destination and committed to sustainable tourism practices. By supporting local communities, you can help preserve cultural heritage and promote economic empowerment.

Respect Nature and Wildlife:

Practice responsible wildlife viewing and conservation during your travels. Avoid activities that exploit or harm animals, such as elephant rides, dolphin shows, or wildlife selfies. Choose eco-friendly wildlife tours and nature excursions that prioritize animal welfare and environmental conservation. Follow Leave No Trace principles and minimize your impact on natural habitats by staying on designated trails, disposing of waste properly, and respecting wildlife habitats.

Reduce, Reuse, Recycle:

Practice waste reduction and recycling wherever you go. Carry a reusable water bottle, shopping bag, and utensils to reduce single-use plastics. Dispose of waste properly and recycle whenever possible, following local recycling guidelines. Participate in beach clean-ups, community recycling initiatives, or environmental conservation projects to give back to the places you visit and leave them better than you found them.

Sustainable travel is about more than just seeing the world – it's about experiencing it in a way that respects and preserves its beauty and diversity. By choosing eco-friendly accommodations, packing light and smart, minimizing carbon emissions, supporting local communities, respecting nature and wildlife, and reducing, reusing, and recycling, we can embark on memorable adventures that benefit the planet and its inhabitants. Let's travel responsibly and inspire others to do the same, creating a more sustainable and equitable world for all.

Alternatives to Car Ownership

While car ownership has long been the norm for personal transportation, it comes with significant costs and environmental impacts. Fortunately, a variety of sustainable alternatives to car ownership are emerging, offering flexibility, affordability, and eco-friendliness. By exploring these alternatives, individuals can reduce their carbon footprint, ease traffic congestion, and promote more sustainable urban mobility.

Public transit systems, including buses, trains, subways, and light rail, provide an efficient and environmentally friendly alternative to car ownership. By consolidating passengers into shared vehicles, public transit reduces the number of cars on the road and decreases greenhouse gas emissions per capita. Additionally, many public transit systems are investing in electrification and renewable energy sources to further reduce their environmental impact. Using public transit not only reduces carbon emissions but also saves money on fuel, parking, and maintenance costs associated with car ownership.

Shared portability administrations, for example, ride-hailing, vehicle sharing, and bicycle sharing, offer advantageous options in contrast to conventional vehicle possession. Ride-hailing services provide on-demand transportation without the need for personal vehicle ownership, reducing the need for parking and decreasing traffic congestion. Car-sharing programs allow users to access vehicles as needed for short-term trips, while bike-sharing programs provide a sustainable and healthy option for urban commuting. By embracing shared mobility services, individuals can reduce their reliance on personal vehicles and contribute to more efficient and sustainable urban mobility.

Walking and cycling are among the most sustainable modes of transportation available, providing health benefits while minimizing environmental impact. Walking and cycling require minimal infrastructure and produce zero emissions, making them ideal options for short trips and urban commuting. Many cities are investing in infrastructure improvements, such as bike lanes, pedestrian-friendly streets, and mixed-use development, to encourage active transportation and create more walk able, bike able communities. By embracing walking and cycling as primary modes of transportation, individuals can reduce their carbon footprint, improve their health, and enjoy a more connected and vibrant urban environment.

Telecommuting and remote work offer an alternative to traditional commuting by allowing individuals to work from home or other remote locations. Remote work reduces the need for daily commuting, saving time, money, and energy associated with transportation. Additionally, remote work can help alleviate traffic congestion, reduce air pollution, and promote work-life balance. With advances in technology and communication tools, many jobs can be performed remotely, providing flexibility and freedom for employees while reducing the environmental impact of commuting.

Community-based transportation initiatives, such as carpooling, vanpooling, and neighbourhood shuttles, offer collaborative solutions to transportation challenges. Carpooling and vanpooling allow individuals to share rides with others travelling in the same direction, reducing the number of vehicles on the road and decreasing carbon emissions. Neighbourhood shuttles provide convenient and affordable transportation options for residents within a community, connecting them to essential services and amenities. By fostering collaboration and community engagement, these initiatives promote more sustainable and inclusive transportation solutions.

Car ownership has long been synonymous with personal mobility, but it's not the only option available. By exploring alternatives such as public transit, shared mobility services, active transportation, telecommuting, and community-based solutions, individuals can reduce their dependence on personal vehicles and embrace more sustainable and efficient modes of transportation. Together, let's rethink mobility and create a future where transportation is accessible, affordable, and eco-friendly for all.

CHAPTER TEN

Building a Sustainable Community

In an era defined by rapid urbanization, climate change, and social inequality, the concept of sustainable communities has gained increasing prominence. Sustainable communities are built on principles of environmental stewardship, social equity, and economic resilience, aiming to create vibrant, liveable spaces for all residents. By embracing sustainability at the local level, communities can improve quality of life, protect natural resources, and foster a sense of belonging and well-being among residents.

At the heart of sustainable communities lies urban planning that prioritizes environmental sustainability, social inclusion, and economic prosperity. Sustainable urban planning seeks to create compact, walk able neighbourhoods with mixed land uses, efficient transportation systems, and access to green spaces and public amenities. By promoting smart growth principles such as transit-oriented development, infill development, and green building practices, communities can reduce sprawl, minimize resource consumption, and enhance quality of life for residents.

Sustainable communities prioritize renewable energy sources and efficient resource management to reduce environmental impact and promote resilience. By investing in renewable energy technologies such as solar, wind, and geothermal power, communities can decrease reliance on fossil fuels and mitigate climate change. Additionally, implementing energy efficiency measures, water conservation strategies, and waste reduction initiatives can further reduce resource consumption and minimize environmental footprint.

Sustainable communities provide residents with accessible, affordable, and eco-friendly transportation options that reduce congestion, improve air quality, and promote public health. Investing in public transit infrastructure, bike lanes, pedestrian-friendly streets, and shared mobility services encourages active transportation and reduces reliance on personal vehicles. By prioritizing transit-oriented development and complete streets design, communities can create safe, inclusive, and connected transportation networks that meet the diverse needs of residents.

Green spaces are essential for sustainable communities, providing recreational opportunities, ecosystem services, and biodiversity conservation. Parks, urban forests, community gardens, and green roofs enhance air and water quality, mitigate urban heat island effects, and promote physical and mental well-being. By preserving and expanding green spaces, communities can create resilient, liveable environments that support ecological diversity and connect people with nature.

Sustainable communities prioritize social equity and inclusion, ensuring that all residents have access to affordable housing, quality education, healthcare, and employment opportunities. Affordable housing policies, mixed-income developments, and equitable land use planning help address housing affordability and combat gentrification and displacement. Additionally, community engagement, participatory decision-making processes, and inclusive public spaces foster a sense of belonging and empower residents to shape the future of their communities.

Sustainable communities support vibrant local economies and resilient food systems that promote economic diversity, food security, and community self-reliance. Investing in local businesses, cooperatives, and social enterprises creates jobs, stimulates economic growth, and builds community wealth. Supporting farmers markets, community-supported agriculture (CSA) programs, and urban agriculture initiatives promotes local food production, reduces food miles, and strengthens community connections.

Building sustainable communities requires collaboration, innovation, and a shared vision for the future. By embracing principles of environmental stewardship, social equity, and economic resilience, communities can create vibrant, liveable spaces that meet the needs of current and future generations. Together, let's build a blueprint for sustainable communities that fosters prosperity, equity, and well-being for all.

Getting Involved Locally

Community involvement is the cornerstone of sustainable development, empowering individuals to make a meaningful impact on local issues and contribute to global sustainability efforts. By getting involved in your community, you can inspire positive change, build connections, and create a more resilient and inclusive future for all. Here are some ways to take action and make a difference in your local area.

Volunteering for local nonprofits, community groups, and environmental organizations is a powerful way to get involved and give back to your community. Whether it's participating in clean-up events, volunteering at a local food bank, or helping out at a community garden, there are countless opportunities to make a difference. Identify organizations that align with your interests and values, and reach out to see how you can contribute your time and skills to meaningful projects and initiatives.

Attend community events, workshops, and forums to learn about local issues and connect with like-minded individuals. Whether it's a neighbourhood meeting, a sustainability workshop, or a climate action rally, participating in community events provides opportunities to engage with others, share ideas, and collaborate on solutions. Look for events hosted by local organizations, government agencies, and grassroots initiatives, and be proactive about getting involved in discussions and activities that matter to you.

Supporting local businesses and initiatives is another impactful way to contribute to your community's sustainability. Choose to shop locally and support businesses that prioritize environmental sustainability, social responsibility, and ethical practices. Look for businesses that source locally, reduce waste, and support community initiatives and events. Additionally, consider investing in local cooperatives, community-supported agriculture (CSA) programs, and social enterprises that contribute to a resilient and inclusive local economy.

Advocacy is a powerful tool for driving positive change in your community. Whether it's advocating for sustainable policies, infrastructure improvements, or environmental protections, speaking up and taking action can make a difference. Write letters to elected officials, attend public meetings, and join advocacy campaigns to voice your concerns and support initiatives that align with sustainability goals. By amplifying your voice and mobilizing others, you can influence decision-making processes and create a more sustainable and equitable community.

Initiate or participate in community projects that address local sustainability challenges and contribute to positive change. Whether it's starting a community garden, organizing a recycling drive, or launching a renewable energy initiative, grassroots projects have the power to transform communities from the ground up. Collaborate with neighbours, local organizations, and government agencies to identify needs and opportunities, and work together to implement solutions that benefit the community and the environment.

Education and awareness are essential components of sustainable community development. Share information and resources with others to raise awareness about environmental issues, social justice, and sustainability solutions. Host workshops, film screenings, and educational events to engage community members and inspire action. By empowering others with knowledge and tools for change, you can mobilize collective action and create a ripple effect of positive impact in your community and beyond.

Getting involved in your community is a powerful way to make a difference and contribute to a more sustainable and equitable future. Whether it's volunteering for local organizations, joining community events, supporting local businesses, advocating for change, starting community projects, or educating and engaging others, there are countless ways to take action and create positive change in your local area. Together, let's harness the power of community involvement to build a more resilient, inclusive, and sustainable world for generations to come.

Community Gardening and Shared Resources

Community gardening and shared resource initiatives are powerful ways to foster connection, promote sustainability, and enhance quality of life within neighbourhoods and communities. By coming together to cultivate shared spaces and resources, community members can not only grow fresh food but also build relationships, share knowledge, and create vibrant, resilient communities. Here's how community gardening and shared resources can transform neighbourhoods and empower residents.

Community gardens provide shared spaces where individuals can come together to grow fruits, vegetables, herbs, and flowers. These green oases not only beautify neighbourhoods but also provide opportunities for recreation, education, and food production. Community members of all ages and backgrounds can participate in planning, planting, tending, and harvesting the garden, fostering a sense of ownership and pride in the shared space. Additionally, community gardens often serve as hubs for social gatherings, workshops, and skill-sharing events, strengthening community bonds and promoting cultural exchange.

Community gardens play a critical role in promoting food security and nutrition by increasing access to fresh, locally grown produce. In neighbourhoods with limited access to healthy food options, community gardens provide an important source of nutritious food, empowering residents to take control of their health and well-being. Additionally, community gardens can serve as educational resources, teaching children and adults about gardening, nutrition, and environmental stewardship. By cultivating and sharing fresh food within the community, gardeners can address food insecurity and promote healthy eating habits for all.

Community gardens are not only spaces for food production but also opportunities to promote environmental stewardship and sustainability. By practicing organic gardening methods, composting organic waste, and conserving water, community gardeners can reduce their environmental footprint and contribute to local ecosystem health. Additionally, community gardens provide habitat for pollinators and wildlife, support biodiversity, and mitigate the urban heat island effect. Through hands-on learning and environmental education, community gardeners can cultivate a deeper appreciation for nature and inspire sustainable behaviours in their communities.

Shared resource initiatives go beyond community gardens to include a wide range of collaborative projects and initiatives that promote resource sharing and mutual support within communities. From tool libraries and seed swaps to community kitchens and skill-sharing networks, these initiatives encourage residents to pool their resources, share their expertise, and support one another in achieving common goals. By sharing resources and knowledge, community members can reduce waste, save money, and build resilience in the face of challenges such as economic hardship, climate change, and natural disasters.

At their core, community gardening and shared resource initiatives are about building social connections and resilience within neighbourhoods and communities. By working together towards common goals, community members forge meaningful relationships, strengthen social networks, and foster a sense of belonging and mutual support. These connections not only enhance individual well-being but also build community resilience, enabling residents to weather adversity and thrive in the face of challenges. Through shared experiences, celebrations, and collective action, community members can create vibrant, inclusive communities where everyone has the opportunity to flourish.

Community gardening and shared resource initiatives offer powerful opportunities for individuals to come together, connect with one another, and create positive change in their neighbourhoods and communities. By cultivating shared spaces, promoting food security and nutrition, fostering environmental stewardship, sharing resources and knowledge, and building social connections and resilience, community members can transform their communities into vibrant, resilient, and sustainable places where everyone has the opportunity to thrive. Together, let's harness the power of community gardening and shared resources to cultivate a brighter, more sustainable future for all.

Organizing and Participating in Local Environmental Initiatives

Local environmental initiatives are essential for addressing pressing environmental challenges and creating more sustainable and resilient communities. By organizing and participating in these initiatives, individuals can make a meaningful impact on the environment, promote sustainability, and inspire positive change within their communities. Here's how to get involved in local environmental initiatives and become a catalyst for environmental stewardship and action.

Identify Local Environmental Issues:

Start by identifying local environmental issues and challenges that need attention in your community. This could include issues such as air and water pollution, waste management, habitat loss, climate change impacts, or environmental justice concerns. Conduct research, engage with community members, and collaborate with local organizations and government agencies to better understand the environmental issues facing your community and prioritize areas for action.

Form or Join Environmental Groups:

Form or join environmental groups, clubs, or organizations in your community to collaborate with like-minded individuals and work towards common environmental goals. These groups provide opportunities to share ideas, expertise, and resources, and to mobilize collective action on local environmental issues. Whether it's a community clean-up crew, a tree planting initiative, or a climate action group, joining forces with others amplifies your impact and fosters a sense of solidarity and purpose.

How to Advocate for Change

Advocating for change is a powerful way to make a positive impact on the world around you, whether it's in your community, your workplace, or on a larger scale. Here's a guide on how to effectively advocate for change:

Start by identifying the issue or cause you're passionate about. Whether it's environmental conservation, social justice, healthcare access, or education reform, choose a cause that aligns with your values and interests.

Take the time to educate yourself about the issue you're advocating for. Research the root causes, consequences, and potential solutions. Stay informed about relevant policies, laws, and current events. Understanding the issue thoroughly will help you make a more compelling case for change.

Set clear, attainable objectives for your advocacy efforts. Determine what specific changes you want to see and how you plan to achieve them. Break down your goals into smaller, actionable steps to keep your advocacy efforts focused and measurable.

Collaborate with like-minded individuals, organizations, and community groups who share your passion for the cause. Building a coalition allows you to amplify your voice, pool resources, and mobilize collective action. Reach out to potential allies, form partnerships, and work together towards common goals.

Speak up and use your voice to advocate for change. Write letters to elected officials, participate in public hearings and town hall meetings, and engage with policymakers and decision-makers. Share your personal story, experiences, and expertise to make a compelling case for why change is needed.

Mobilize support for your cause by raising awareness and rallying public support. Use social media, traditional media, and grassroots outreach to spread the word, educate others, and build momentum for change. Organize events, rallies, marches, and petition drives to mobilize supporters and demonstrate public demand for action.

Advocating for change is often a long and challenging process, requiring patience, persistence, and resilience. Stay committed to your cause and be prepared to face obstacles and setbacks along the way. Celebrate small victories, learn from setbacks, and keep pushing forward towards your goals.

Engage in constructive dialogue with stakeholders, decision-makers, and opponents to build consensus and find common ground. Listen actively, be respectful, and seek to understand differing perspectives. Find opportunities for collaboration and compromise where possible while staying true to your core values and goals.

Monitor progress towards your advocacy goals and track the impact of your efforts. Keep tabs on relevant policies, legislation, and developments related to your cause. Measure success by evaluating outcomes, assessing impact, and adjusting strategies as needed to stay effective and relevant.

Keep morale high and maintain momentum by celebrating milestones and successes along the way. Recognize the contributions of individuals and groups who have helped advance the cause. Use successes as opportunities to inspire others, attract new supporters, and build towards larger, long-term goals.

By following these steps and staying committed to your cause, you can become an effective advocate for change and make a meaningful difference in the world. Remember that change takes time, but every voice and action matters in the journey towards a better, more just, and sustainable future.

Joining Environmental Organizations

Joining environmental organizations is a fantastic way to channel your passion for the environment into meaningful action. Here's a guide on how to find and join the right environmental organization for you:

Start by researching environmental organizations that align with your interests, values, and goals. Consider the scope of their work, their mission and values, their track record of accomplishments, and their approach to environmental issues. Look for organizations that focus on specific areas of environmental conservation, advocacy, education, or activism that resonate with you.

Explore both local and global environmental organizations to find opportunities for involvement in your community and beyond. Local organizations may focus on issues such as urban sustainability, wildlife conservation, or environmental education in your area, while global organizations may work on broader issues like climate change, biodiversity conservation, or environmental justice on a larger scale.

Consider your skills, interests, and strengths when choosing an environmental organization to join. Think about how you can best contribute to the organization's mission and goals based on your background, expertise, and interests. Whether you're passionate about scientific research, community organizing, policy advocacy, communications, or fundraising, there's likely a role for you within an environmental organization.

Attend events, meetings, and activities hosted by environmental organizations to learn more about their work and meet members and volunteers. Many organizations hold regular meetings, workshops, volunteer opportunities, and social events that provide opportunities for networking, learning, and engagement. Participating in these events allows you to get a sense of the organization's culture, values, and community of supporters.

Volunteer your time and skills to support the work of environmental organizations. Many organizations rely on volunteers to help with a variety of tasks, such as organizing events, conducting research, writing articles, designing graphics, managing social media, or participating in conservation projects. Volunteering not only allows you to contribute to the organization's mission but also provides valuable opportunities for skill development, networking, and personal growth.

Consider becoming a formal member of an environmental organization to show your support and commitment to their mission. Membership may come with benefits such as voting rights, discounts on events or merchandise, access to exclusive resources or opportunities, and opportunities to get involved in leadership roles within the organization. Membership fees or dues may apply, but they often help support the organization's programs and activities.

Stay informed and engaged with the work of the environmental organization you join. Keep up-to-date on their campaigns, initiatives, and events through their website, newsletters, social media channels, and other communication channels. Participate in meetings, discussions, and decision-making processes within the organization to have a voice in shaping its direction and priorities.

Connect with like-minded individuals who share your passion for the environment through the organization's networks and communities. Build relationships with fellow members, volunteers, staff, and supporters who can provide support, inspiration, and camaraderie as you work together towards common goals. Collaborate with others to amplify your impact and make a difference in the world.

By joining environmental organizations, you can connect with others who share your passion for the environment, contribute to meaningful projects and initiatives, and make a positive impact on the planet. Choose organizations that align with your values and interests, and get involved in ways that leverage your skills and expertise to support their mission.

CHAPTER ELEVEN

Greening Your Workplace

Creating a sustainable workplace is not only beneficial for the environment but also for employee well-being, company reputation, and cost savings. Greening your workplace involves implementing practices and policies that reduce environmental impact, conserve resources, and promote a culture of sustainability. Here's a comprehensive guide on how to make your office more eco-friendly and sustainable.

Conduct a Sustainability Audit:

Start by conducting a sustainability audit to assess your current environmental impact and identify areas for improvement. Evaluate energy consumption, water usage, waste management, transportation practices, and office supplies. This audit will provide a baseline for measuring progress and help prioritize initiatives.

Implement Energy-Efficient Practices:

Utilize energy-saving technologies and practices to cut down on energy use:

- Switch to LED lighting and install motion sensors to reduce energy use in unoccupied spaces.

- Encourage the use of natural light by keeping windows clean and using light-coloured paint.

- Make an investment in office equipment and appliances that save energy.

- Promote a culture of turning off lights, computers, and other equipment when not in use.

Reduce, Reuse, Recycle:

- Minimize waste and promote recycling within the office:

- Set up clearly labelled recycling bins for paper, plastic, glass, and electronic waste.

- Encourage double-sided printing and the use of digital documents to reduce paper consumption.

- Implement a policy for reusing office supplies, such as binders, folders, and envelopes.

- Partner with e-waste recycling programs for proper disposal of electronic equipment.

Promote Sustainable Transportation:

Encourage employees to adopt sustainable transportation methods:

- Offer incentives for carpooling, public transit, biking, or walking to work.
- Provide secure bike storage and shower facilities for employees who bike to work.
- Implement a remote work policy to reduce commuting emissions.
- Consider providing electric vehicle charging stations if feasible.

Conserve Water:

Implement water-saving measures to reduce water consumption:

- Install low-flow faucets and toilets in restrooms.
- Encourage workers to report leaks and promptly fix them.
- Use drought-resistant plants and smart irrigation systems for any landscaping.
- Source Sustainable Office Supplies:

Choose eco-friendly office supplies and materials:

- Purchase recycled paper and other office products made from sustainable materials.

- Use non-toxic, environmentally friendly cleaning supplies.

- Choose furniture and fixtures made from recycled or sustainable materials.

- Foster a Culture of Sustainability:

- Engage employees in sustainability initiatives and promote a culture of environmental responsibility:

- Form a green team or sustainability committee to lead and coordinate efforts.

- Organize regular sustainability workshops, training, and awareness campaigns.

- Encourage employee suggestions and involvement in sustainability projects.

- Celebrate and reward sustainable practices and achievements within the office.

Implement Green Policies and Practices:

Establish formal policies and practices to institutionalize sustainability:

- Develop a sustainability policy that outlines the company's commitment to environmental stewardship.
- Set specific, measurable sustainability goals and track progress regularly.
- Integrate sustainability criteria into procurement processes and vendor selection.
- Implement a green meeting policy that encourages virtual meetings, paperless agendas, and sustainable catering options.

Monitor and Report Progress:

Regularly monitor and report on sustainability initiatives and achievements:

- Use sustainability metrics and key performance indicators (KPIs) to track progress.

- Publish an annual sustainability report to communicate efforts and outcomes to employees, stakeholders, and customers.
- Continuously seek feedback and identify areas for further improvement.

Greening your workplace requires a collective effort and commitment from all levels of the organization. By implementing energy-efficient practices, reducing waste, promoting sustainable transportation, conserving water, sourcing eco-friendly supplies, fostering a culture of sustainability, establishing green policies, and monitoring progress, you can create a more sustainable and eco-friendly workplace. Together, let's take steps towards a greener future and make a positive impact on the environment.

Encouraging a Green Office Culture

Cultivating a green office culture is essential for fostering sustainability and environmental responsibility within the workplace. A green office culture not only benefits the planet but also enhances employee morale, productivity, and corporate image. Here's a comprehensive guide to encouraging a green office culture and making sustainability a core part of your organization's identity.

Leadership plays a crucial role in shaping office culture. When executives and managers demonstrate a commitment to sustainability, it sets a powerful example for employees to follow. Leaders should actively participate in green initiatives, make environmentally responsible decisions, and communicate the importance of sustainability to the entire organization.

Educate employees about the importance of sustainability and the specific environmental goals of the organization. Provide training sessions, workshops, and informational resources that cover topics such as energy conservation, waste reduction, and sustainable practices. Raising awareness helps employees understand their role in achieving the organization's sustainability objectives.

Establish clear sustainability goals and policies that align with your organization's mission and values. Communicate these goals to all employees and integrate them into daily operations. Policies could include guidelines for energy use, waste management, transportation, and procurement.

Clear goals and policies provide a framework for consistent and coordinated action.

Engage employees in sustainability initiatives by creating opportunities for participation and input. Form green teams or sustainability committees that include representatives from various departments. Encourage employees to suggest ideas, lead projects, and take ownership of specific initiatives. Employee involvement fosters a sense of responsibility and commitment to sustainability.

Promote Sustainable Commuting:

- Encourage employees to adopt eco-friendly commuting options:
- Offer incentives for carpooling, public transportation, biking, or walking to work.
- Provide facilities such as bike racks and showers for cyclists.
- Implement flexible working hours or telecommuting policies to reduce commuting emissions.

Implement a robust waste management program that focuses on reducing, reusing, and recycling:

- Set up clearly labelled recycling stations for paper, plastic, glass, and electronic waste.
- Encourage the use of digital documents to reduce paper consumption.
- Promote the reuse of office supplies and equipment.
- Organize office-wide recycling drives and events to raise awareness and encourage participation.

Adopt practices that conserve energy and water in the workplace:

- Use energy-efficient lighting and appliances.
- Urge representatives to switch out lights, PCs, and other gear when not being used.
- To save water, install toilets and faucets with low flow rates.
- Conduct regular energy and water audits to identify and address inefficiencies.

Choose eco-friendly products and services for your office:

- Get office supplies that are made of recycled or renewable materials.
- Use non-toxic, eco-friendly cleaning products.

- Work with suppliers and vendors who place a high value on sustainability.
- Consider the environmental impact of purchases and prioritize quality and durability over disposable items.

Recognize and reward employees and teams for their contributions to sustainability:

- Implement a recognition program that highlights sustainable practices and achievements.
- Celebrate milestones and successes with events, awards, and public acknowledgment.
- Share stories and case studies of sustainability efforts to inspire and motivate others.

Encourage collaboration and knowledge sharing among employees:

- Create platforms for employees to share ideas, best practices, and success stories.
- Organize regular meetings and discussions focused on sustainability topics.
- Foster a culture of continuous improvement and innovation in sustainability practices.

Encouraging a green office culture requires commitment, education, and active participation from all levels of the organization. By leading by example, setting clear goals, involving employees, promoting sustainable commuting, managing waste, conserving resources, implementing sustainable procurement, celebrating achievements, and fostering collaboration, your organization can build a vibrant and effective green office culture. Together, let's create a workplace environment that prioritizes sustainability and makes a positive impact on the planet.

Remote Work and Its Environmental Benefits

Remote work has become an increasingly popular and viable work model, especially in light of recent global events. Beyond its advantages for work-life balance and productivity, remote work also offers significant environmental benefits. By reducing the need for daily commutes, lowering office resource consumption, and minimizing the carbon footprint, remote work contributes to a more sustainable future. Here is the environmental benefits of remote work and how organizations can maximize these advantages.

Reduced Commuting Emissions:

Fewer Cars on the Road: With fewer employees commuting daily, there are fewer cars on the road, which leads to a reduction in traffic congestion and greenhouse gas emissions.

Lower Fuel Consumption: Reduced commuting results in lower fuel consumption, which decreases the demand for fossil fuels and helps mitigate air pollution.

Decreased Public Transportation Use: While public transportation is generally more sustainable than individual car use, reduced demand can still lead to lower overall energy consumption and emissions.

Lower Office Energy Consumption:

Remote work reduces the energy consumption associated with maintaining a physical office space:

Heating and Cooling: With fewer employees in the office, energy use for heating and cooling buildings can be significantly reduced.

Lighting: Reduced occupancy means less energy is needed for lighting during working hours.

Office Equipment: Fewer people in the office also means reduced use of office equipment such as computers, printers, and copiers, leading to lower overall energy consumption.

Decreased Office Waste:

Remote work minimizes the generation of office waste:

Paper Use: Remote work often leads to a greater reliance on digital documents and communication, reducing the need for printed materials and paper waste.

Disposable Items: With fewer employees on-site, there is less demand for disposable items such as coffee cups, plastic utensils, and food packaging.

General Waste: A reduction in the number of people using office facilities results in less overall waste from office operations.

Encouraging Sustainable Practices at Home:

Remote work can encourage employees to adopt more sustainable practices in their home offices:

Energy-Efficient Appliances: Employees can be encouraged to use energy-efficient appliances and home office equipment.

Renewable Energy: Remote work can incentivize employees to invest in renewable energy sources, such as solar panels, for their homes.

Waste Reduction: Employees may adopt more sustainable waste management practices, such as recycling and composting, in their home environments.

Reduced Demand for Office Space:

With more employees working remotely, organizations may reduce their demand for office space, leading to environmental benefits:

Smaller Office Footprints: Companies can downsize their physical office spaces, reducing the environmental impact of construction, maintenance, and utilities.

Sustainable Building Practices: Organizations can invest in sustainable building practices and energy-efficient designs for any remaining office spaces.

Flexible Work Schedules and Sustainability:

Remote work offers flexibility that can further enhance sustainability:

Off-Peak Energy Use: Employees working from home can stagger their work hours to avoid peak energy demand times, reducing strain on the energy grid.

Efficient Resource Use: Flexibility in work schedules allows for more efficient use of resources, as employees can plan their work around the most sustainable practices.

Remote work presents a compelling opportunity for organizations to reduce their environmental impact and promote sustainability. By minimizing commuting emissions, lowering office energy consumption, decreasing waste, encouraging sustainable home practices, reducing the demand for office space, and offering flexible work schedules, remote work can significantly contribute to a more sustainable future.

As organizations continue to adapt to new work models, embracing remote work as part of a broader sustainability strategy can help create a greener and more resilient world.

Together, let's leverage the environmental benefits of remote work to build a more sustainable and environmentally responsible workplace.

CHAPTER TWELVE

The Environmental Impact of Digital Technology

Digital technology has revolutionized the way we live, work, and communicate, bringing numerous benefits such as increased efficiency, connectivity, and access to information. However, the environmental impact of digital technology is significant and often overlooked. From energy consumption to electronic waste, digital technology poses several challenges to sustainability. This chapter explores the environmental impact of digital technology and offers strategies for mitigating these effects.

Digital technology consumes vast amounts of energy, contributing to carbon emissions and climate change. Data centres, which store and manage vast amounts of digital information, require substantial energy for operation and cooling. These centres are significant contributors to global energy consumption.

The production, use, and charging of digital devices (smart phones, tablets, laptops, etc.) also consume considerable energy. The increasing demand for these devices amplifies their environmental impact.

The rapid pace of technological advancement leads to a high turnover of digital devices, resulting in substantial electronic waste. Many digital devices end up in landfills, where toxic substances like lead, mercury, and cadmium can leach into the environment, causing soil and water pollution.

Recycling e-waste is complex and often inefficient. Recovering valuable materials from devices requires specialized processes, and not all e-waste is properly recycled.

The production of digital technology requires significant amounts of raw materials, many of which are finite and sourced through environmentally damaging methods. Extracting minerals such as gold, silver, and rare earth elements for use in digital devices often involves harmful mining practices that destroy ecosystems and pollute water sources.

The manufacturing process of digital devices consumes water and energy and emits pollutants, further exacerbating environmental degradation.

The use of digital technology contributes to an individual's or organization's carbon footprint. Activities such as streaming videos, online gaming, and cloud computing require energy-intensive data centres and networks, leading to increased carbon emissions. The global infrastructure supporting the internet, including servers, networks, and data centres, has a substantial carbon footprint.

Strategies for Mitigating the Environmental Impact of Digital Technology:

Encourage the use of energy-efficient technologies and practices in data centres, such as optimizing cooling systems, using renewable energy sources, and improving server utilization rates.

Advocate for the production and use of energy-efficient digital devices. Encourage manufacturers to design devices that consume less power and support users in adopting energy-saving habits, such as turning off devices when not in use.

Support and participate in e-waste recycling programs. Ensure that digital devices are disposed of properly and that valuable materials are recovered and reused.

Extended Producer Responsibility: Advocate for policies that hold manufacturers accountable for the entire lifecycle of their products, including take-back and recycling programs.

Promote and support ethical mining practices that minimize environmental damage and protect local communities. Seek certification and transparency from suppliers regarding their sourcing practices.

Encourage manufacturers to adopt sustainable practices, such as reducing water and energy consumption, minimizing waste, and using recycled materials.

Adopt sustainable digital practices, such as reducing unnecessary data storage, optimizing website performance, and using cloud services efficiently.

Support and invest in renewable energy sources for powering digital infrastructure. Encourage the tech industry to transition to renewable energy to reduce the carbon footprint of digital technology.

Educate consumers about the environmental impact of digital technology and the importance of sustainable practices. Encourage responsible purchasing decisions and the use of energy-efficient devices.

Foster collaboration within the tech industry to share best practices, develop sustainable technologies, and advocate for policies that promote environmental responsibility.

While digital technology offers numerous benefits, it also presents significant environmental challenges. By promoting energy efficiency, managing e-waste responsibly, supporting sustainable sourcing, reducing the digital carbon footprint, and raising awareness, we can mitigate the environmental impact of digital technology. Balancing progress with sustainability requires collective action from individuals, organizations, and the tech industry to create a greener and more sustainable future. Together, let's harness the power of digital technology while protecting the planet for future generations.

Sustainable Practices for the Digital Age

In a world where technology reigns supreme, our digital footprint has become as significant as the ones we leave on the earth. As we marvel at the wonders of the digital age, it's crucial to remember that our actions in the virtual realm have real-world consequences. But fear not, for amidst the sea of data and innovation, there shines a beacon of hope—a roadmap to sustainability in the digital age.

Picture a future where every click, every tap, and every download is a step towards a greener tomorrow. This is the vision of sustainable practices for the digital age—a vision where technology and environmental stewardship intertwine to create a world where progress is synonymous with preservation.

At the heart of this vision lies the quest for energy efficiency. From the sleek smart phones in our pockets to the towering data centres that power the internet, optimizing energy usage is paramount. By choosing energy-efficient devices, embracing renewable energy sources, and practicing mindful power management, we can minimize our digital carbon footprint and pave the way for a more sustainable future.

But sustainability in the digital age extends beyond mere energy conservation—it's about reimagining the entire lifecycle of our digital devices. Imagine a world where electronic waste is a relic of the past, where every gadget is designed for durability, reparability, and eventual repurposing. By investing in quality products, supporting refurbishment programs, and recycling old electronics responsibly, we can breathe new life into our digital companions and reduce the environmental impact of our technological pursuits.

Yet, sustainability in the digital age is not just about hardware—it's also about the invisible infrastructure that powers our online world. From the vast expanses of cloud storage to the endless streams of digital data, managing our digital footprint responsibly is essential. By optimizing data storage, practicing digital minimalism, and embracing green hosting solutions, we can minimize the environmental impact of our online activities and ensure that our digital infrastructure is as sustainable as it is innovative.

But perhaps the most transformative aspect of sustainable practices for the digital age lies in the realm of innovation. As we push the boundaries of technology, we have the power to shape a future where sustainability is not just a goal but a fundamental principle of design. From eco-friendly software development practices to the embrace of emerging technologies like block chain and artificial intelligence for environmental conservation, the possibilities are limitless.

In the end, sustainable practices for the digital age are not just about preserving the planet—it's about embracing a new paradigm of progress. It's about recognizing that our digital actions have real-world consequences and using technology as a force for good. It's about charting a course towards a future where innovation and sustainability go hand in hand—a future where the digital frontier is not just a realm of endless possibility, but a sign of hope for future generations.

Minimizing E-Waste: Strategies for a Sustainable Digital Future

In the heart of every Smartphone, laptop, and tablet lies a story—a tale of innovation, connection, and endless possibilities. But amidst the marvels of our digital age, there's a darker narrative unfolding—one of waste, pollution, and environmental degradation. Electronic waste, or e-waste, is mounting at an alarming rate, threatening our planet and its delicate ecosystems. Yet, in the face of this crisis, there shines a beacon of hope—a vision of a sustainable digital future, where technology and environmental stewardship intertwine to create a world where progress is synonymous with preservation.

Imagine a world where electronic devices are not disposable commodities but cherished companions, designed with longevity and reparability in mind. This is the first step towards minimizing e-waste—reimagining the lifecycle of our gadgets. By prioritizing durability and reparability in product design, we can ensure that our devices stand the test of time, becoming cherished heirlooms rather than fleeting fads.

But our journey towards sustainability does not end there. We must also embrace the concept of extended product lifecycles, breathing new life into old electronics through software updates and modular design.

With regular updates and upgradability, our devices can evolve alongside us, remaining relevant and functional for years to come. It's a paradigm shift—a departure from the culture of disposability towards a future where every device has the potential for enduring relevance.

Yet, in our quest for sustainability, we cannot ignore the power of reuse and refurbishment. Just as one man's trash can be another's treasure, so too can our discarded electronics find new purpose through refurbishment programs and donation initiatives. By giving old devices a second chance at life, we not only reduce e-waste but also extend the reach of technology to those in need, fostering digital inclusion and empowerment.

Of course, responsible recycling remains a cornerstone of our sustainable digital future. By partnering with certified e-waste recyclers and establishing take-back programs, we can ensure that every device reaches its end-of-life with dignity, with its precious materials reclaimed and repurposed for future generations. It's a virtuous cycle—a testament to the resilience of our planet and the ingenuity of human innovation.

Yet, amidst the clamour for change, education emerges as our most potent weapon. Through awareness campaigns and consumer guidance, we can empower individuals to make informed decisions about their electronics, guiding them towards responsible disposal practices and ethical purchasing choices. It's a ripple effect—a ripple that has the power to transform our world, one gadget at a time.

But perhaps our greatest ally in the fight against e-waste is innovation itself. As we embrace the principles of the circular economy and explore alternative business models, such as product-as-a-service, we unlock new pathways towards sustainability, where waste becomes a relic of the past and resource efficiency reigns supreme. It's a revolution—a revolution that heralds a new era of possibility, where progress is no longer at odds with the planet but intertwined with its very essence.

In the end, our journey towards a sustainable digital future is not just about saving the planet—it's about preserving the stories contained within every device, the memories etched in every line of code. It's about unlocking the potential of technology to uplift and empower, to connect and inspire. It's about embracing a future where progress is synonymous with preservation—a future where every device, every innovation, every step forward is a testament to the resilience of the human spirit and the enduring beauty of our planet.

CONCLUSION

As we stand at the intersection of progress and preservation, it's essential to take a moment to reflect on our sustainable journey—the path we've travelled, the challenges we've faced, and the milestones we've achieved. From the early days of awareness to the ongoing commitment to change, our journey towards sustainability has been a testament to the power of collective action and shared responsibility.

Reflecting on our sustainable journey, we are reminded of the small steps that have led to significant strides. From the decision to reduce energy consumption in our daily lives to the conscious effort to minimize waste and embrace eco-friendly practices, each choice has been a step towards a greener, more sustainable future. It's a journey marked by learning and growth, where every challenge has been met with resilience and determination.

Be that as it may, the way to supportability is not even close to finished. As we continue to navigate the complexities of the modern world, it's crucial to renew our commitment to the planet—to double down on our efforts and push forward with even greater resolve. For the challenges we face are daunting, but the potential for change is boundless.

Continuing our commitment to the planet means embracing new opportunities and innovative solutions. It means exploring new technologies and embracing sustainable practices in every aspect of our lives. From the way we consume energy to the products we buy and the companies we support, every decision we make has the power to shape the world we live in.

But perhaps most importantly, continuing our commitment to the planet means recognizing that sustainability is not just a goal to be achieved but a journey to be embraced. It's about fostering a mindset of stewardship and responsibility—a recognition that we are all custodians of this planet and that the choices we make today will impact future generations for years to come.

So let us continue our sustainable journey with renewed purpose and determination. Let us embrace the challenges that lie ahead and seize the opportunities to create a brighter, more sustainable future for all. For together, we can build a world where progress and preservation go hand in hand—a world where the planet thrives, and future generations can flourish.

Appendix

Checklist for a Sustainable Lifestyle

Living sustainably is not just a choice; it's a lifestyle—a commitment to making mindful decisions that benefit both ourselves and the planet we call home. To help you embark on your journey towards a more sustainable lifestyle, here's a comprehensive checklist of actions you can take:

Energy Conservation:

- Turn off lights, appliances, and electronics when not in use.
- Switch to energy-efficient LED light bulbs.
- Set your thermostat to an energy-saving temperature.
- Invest in renewable energy sources like solar panels or wind turbines.

Reduce, Reuse, Recycle:

- Minimize single-use plastics by using reusable bags, bottles, and containers.
- Opt for products with minimal packaging or packaging made from recycled materials.

- Recycle paper, glass, metal, and plastic waste whenever possible.
- Donate or sell items you no longer need instead of throwing them away.

Water Conservation:

- Fix leaks and install water-saving fixtures like low-flow toilets and showerheads.
- Take shorter showers and turn off the tap while brushing teeth or washing dishes.
- Collect rainwater for outdoor use and landscaping.

Sustainable Eating:

- Choose locally grown, organic, and seasonal produce when shopping for groceries.
- Reduce meat consumption and incorporate more plant-based meals into your diet.
- Support sustainable seafood options and avoid overfished species.
- Minimize food waste by meal planning, proper storage, and composting organic scraps.

Transportation:

- Walk, bike, or use public transportation whenever possible.
- Carpool or use ride-sharing services to reduce emissions from individual vehicles.
- Choose fuel-efficient or electric vehicles for longer trips or daily commutes.

Green Living at Home:

- Use eco-friendly cleaning products or make your own with natural ingredients like vinegar and baking soda.
- Opt for energy-efficient appliances and electronics with high ENERGY STAR ratings.
- Plant native species in your garden to attract pollinators and support local biodiversity.

Reduce Carbon Footprint:

- Offset your carbon emissions by investing in carbon offset projects or planting trees.
- Support companies and brands that prioritize sustainability and ethical practices.

- Reduce air travel and choose eco-friendly transportation options whenever possible.

Community Engagement:

- Get involved in local environmental initiatives, clean-up events, or community gardens.

- Advocate for sustainable policies and practices in your local government and community organizations.

- Educate others about the importance of sustainability and encourage them to join you on your journey.